Veld to Fork

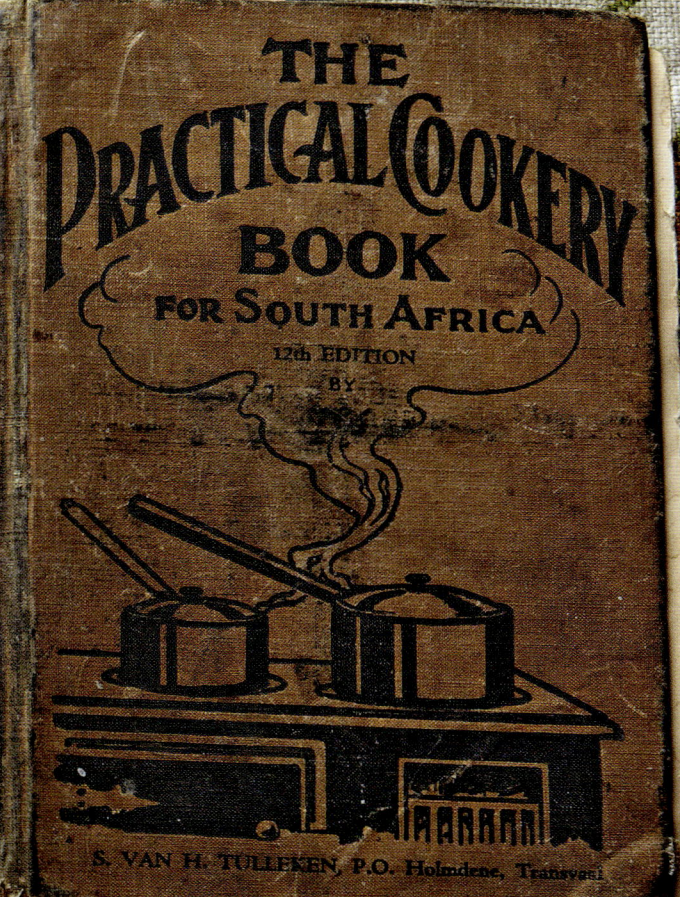

Veld to Fork

Slow food from the heart of the Karoo

Gordon Wright

Photography by Sean Calitz   Styling by Brita du Plessis

Acknowledgements

A few heartfelt thank you's to everyone who made this dream a reality.
Firstly, Linda De Villiers, that doyen of publishing, who saw my vision and believed in it.
My editor, Joy Clack, who helped to shape the words that penned my vision. Bev Dodd and the
creative team of Brita, Yvette and Sean, who did such an amazing job of helping me turn that
vision and dream into this wonderful creation you have before you.
I need to also thank my lovely wife Rose and my two sons, Jason and Max for
putting up with all the late nights and away time.
Roche van As, my brother from another mother, who has always inspired me to
cook and cook well and, of course, to my own mom and all those Karoo moms and
Ousies out there who lit that first cooking fire in my heart as a child.
Lastly, every one of our friends and family (not necessarily all featured in
this book) who have walked this Karoo path with us and have been the true
friends one can only find in the Great Karoo.

It's better to have shot and missed, than never to have shot at all …

Published in 2013 by Struik Lifestyle
an imprint of Random House Struik (Pty) Ltd
Company Reg. No. 1966/003153/07
Wembley Square, 1st Floor,
Solan Street, Gardens 8001
P O Box 1144, Cape Town 8000, South Africa

Visit www.randomstruik.co.za
and subscribe to our newsletter for
monthly updates and news.

Copyright © in published edition:
Random House Struik (Pty) Ltd 2013
Copyright © in text: Gordon Wright 2013
Copyright © in photographs: Random House
Struik (Pty) Ltd 2013, except pages 6, 82 and 83

Reproduction by Hirt & Carter Cape (Pty) Ltd
Printed and bound by 1010 Printing
International Ltd, China

All rights reserved. No part of this
publication may be reproduced, stored
in a retrieval system or transmitted, in any
form or by any means, electronic, mechanical,
photocopying, recording or otherwise,
without the prior written permission
of the publishers and copyright holders.

10 9 8 7 6 5 4 3 2 1

PUBLISHER: Linda de Villiers
MANAGING EDITOR: Cecilia Barfield
EDITOR AND INDEXER: Joy Clack
DESIGNER: Beverley Dodd
PHOTOGRAPHER: Sean Calitz
STYLIST: Brita du Plessis
STYLIST'S ASSISTANT: Yvette Pascoe
PROOFREADER: Samantha Fick

ISBN 978 1 43230 093 7

Contents

About the author 6

The Karoo, Graaff-Reinet and its people 10

Soups 17

Meat 27
Karoo Lamb and Mutton 28
Nguni Beef 46
Free-range Chicken 64
Venison, Furred and Fowl 82
Charcuterie and Deli Cuts 104

Sides and vegetables 119

Dessert in the desert 137

Preserves and baked treats 149

Recipe index 159

About the author

I entered this world in the early 1970s, in the coastal city of Port Elizabeth, the last born in a family of ten. Imagine my poor parents raising five sons and three daughters!

Growing up 'the baby' in such a large family forces you to stand up and fend for yourself from a very young age. This I did, with varying degrees of success, as one can imagine. The one thing I was always very particular about was my food.

I was not a fussy eater, but I have always been very particular about the quality of the food and the preparation (the eggs had to be fried perfectly and presented well – you know how it is). At just two years of age (and many shoddy eggs later), I took charge of the frying pan and decided it would be better to fry my own eggs to ensure a satisfactory result and thus fewer tears from both myself and my long-suffering mother.

Elizabeth Notwala (*see pic on right*), my nanny who helped raise me and often cooked food for my family, had an enormous influence on helping to develop my adventurous pallet. She introduced me to traditional Xhosa dishes like offal, samp and beans (*umngqusho*) and morogo, and I loved exploring the range of flavours, textures and aromas that this added to my otherwise typical Eastern Cape diet of fish, meat, potatoes and veg.

Growing up in the leafy old suburb of Walmer, Port Elizabeth (PE to those who live there) during the 1970s and '80s meant that the annual Walmer town fair and agricultural show was a large part of my life in those days.

I started taking part in the baking competitions from around age six. After taking first prize for my shortbread for three years in a row, I decided to take on the big guns and entered the highly contested chocolate cake competition. No easy feat considering my own Mom had been the undisputed chocolate cake champion for a number of years. Competing against formidable bakers like my mother and around 100 or so established (adult) bakers from the area, this cocky nine year old was the shock

winner with 'an inspiringly rich and moist offering' (as the judges put it).

I walked away with a handsome trophy and the grand prize, much to my mother's pride (and dismay) and evidently the chagrin of the rest of the adult competitors, as the following year it was decided that there should be a separate entry for children. The experience, however, had a lasting effect: this young cook had quite literally tasted success and was never to look back.

Like most kids, my early teen years proved to be a difficult time. The pressures of being at a big city school coupled with a tumultuous relationship with my abusive father added to the stresses of being a typical teenager. The resultant poor academics and social ills were, I suppose, mandatory.

At the end of my STD 7 (Grade 9) year, which I failed handsomely, my exasperated mother shipped me off to boarding school. Despite strongly disagreeing at the time, being sent to The Union High School in the picturesque and very rural little town of Graaff-Reinet, in the heart of the Great Karoo, had a massively positive impact on me, and my culinary love affair was rekindled.

Nestled in the bosom of the Karoo heartland, I was exposed to traditional Karoo *boerekos* (farm food) – organic in the truest sense of the word – homemade EVERYTHING, from the bread and butter to the tomato sauce, to the onion marmalade on the roasted vegetables that had still been growing earlier that morning. The meat, milk and vegetables all came from the garden or, at worst, the neighbour's garden. Food was an enormous part of these Karoo families' lives and meal times were spent together, either outside in the warm sunshine or indoors around the table (always set formally). These memories had a huge impact on me and created a yearning to continue these wonderful food-based traditions that seem to be slipping away in our busy modern lifestyle.

When I was finishing school in the early '90s, my dilemma then was that I had been accepted to study culinary arts in Cape Town, as well as a law degree at the then University of Port Elizabeth. What to do, what to do? Cooking was my first love, but I had also become a bit of an academic (read 'nerd') since my relocation to the Karoo, so it was quite a tough choice.

I decided that a bit of vacation work in the kitchen of a large city hotel should help confirm my choice to become a chef. Two weeks and about 1 million peeled potatoes later, I had made my choice. Much to my parents' delight, the former delinquent opted for a career in law and off to the University of Port Elizabeth I went, where I discovered the joys of student life, rowing, parties, lovely girls and the occasional beer.

I even waded into the shallow end of the pool of culinary arts by way of residence food. My most memorable recollections of fine dining during my student years are bowls of stodgy microwave pasta and sauce washed down with a few cold beers at 2 a.m. on any given Saturday morning after a hard night of partying.

All this time there was a petite, strong-minded and unbelievably beautiful strawberry blonde waiting in the wings (I had met her in my first year at Union High, but she had refused to kiss me) and unbeknownst to both of us, she was to change my life in ways I could not imagine.

Rosemarie van der Merwe was born in the Eastern Cape, the second youngest daughter of a dairy farmer. Near the end of my second year at varsity, shortly after we started courting, this wholesome farm girl started having an unexpected influence on me. I'll let Rose tell this part ...

Rose: Not long into our courtship I realised that Gordon needed some re-education regarding food. At that stage I was working on a private game farm near Grahamstown that was pretty much out in the sticks. When he visited on weekends I would often ask him to bring along some groceries: butter, fresh roasted coffee beans and fresh vegetables [and cigarettes – Gordon].

When he arrived with margarine, instant coffee and a bag of frozen pre-prepped mixed veg [and no cigarettes – Gordon], let's just say that he did not receive the warm reception he was anticipating.

Fortunately, he is fairly bright and very soon his memory reverted to his school days in the Karoo. Whole fresh foods became the order of the day and his visits received a much better reception. He even convinced me to give up smoking. A good trade off I would say.

As our relationship grew, I was furthering my studies in reflexology and becoming more conscious of the health impacts that food had on the human body. I soon started to insist on knowing where food, particularly meat, came from and what had gone into it. Luckily, Gordon was always a keen hunter and fisherman.

After we got married, we could be found, most evenings, cooking up a storm in the kitchen with whatever meagre reserves we could scratch together. In fact, I'm sure all our friends will agree that our kitchen has always been the epicentre of our home.

After five years of married life we decided it was time to start a family. Once the boys were born we became even more health conscious as we both wanted them to grow up accustomed to eating a good, healthy and balanced diet. Young Jason and Max were fed at least three fresh vegetables and two fruits daily as a simple rule.

Cynthia Notwala, Elizabeth's daughter, started working for us when Jason was just six months old. She was also a fabulous cook and understood the importance of a healthy diet.

Gordon soon built an extra long garage with a 16 m² cold room, fully equipped with all the butchery equipment available to prepare any meat he brought home from a hunt. Both of us were formally employed during the day

so at night, once the boys were safely tucked into bed and sound asleep, we churned out sausages, biltong, salami and all sorts of wonderful meat products.

All the while Gordon had been building a career as an investment banker. He was a regional head at a private bank and did a lot of travelling, meaning he was away on business for most of the year.

As the years progressed and the boys grew up, we had to make a decision about their education. Union High had had such a positive influence on Gordon and we were both deeply in love with the Karoo, so we were contemplating sending them to boarding school when they got to high school. As it was, we would escape to the Karoo to visit friends whenever we could get away.

Back to Gordon …

At the end of 2007 the Wright family planned a weekend trip to Graaff-Reinet. The idea was to look for a 'fixer upper' property that could become our base when the boys reached high school. The plan was for Rose to move her therapy practice there and the boys could attend the Union schools. I would continue working and commute.

The food gods, however, had other ideas.

On the weekend involved, the estate agent showed us, it seemed, every single property on the market in Graaff-Reinet at the time. By lunch time on the Saturday we were exhausted, hot, bothered and sick and tired of house 'bloody' hunting!

The agent then asked if we would like to see a guest-house and restaurant that was also available. Hoping this would be the last stop, we reluctantly agreed, quietly plotting our escape along the way. We walked into the Andries Stockenström Guest House and Restaurant and before we were even past the entrance foyer we were sold.

There were, however, a few problems.

Foremost of these were that the price was way above our range and we had never (ever!) owned or run a guesthouse or restaurant.

I had been doing plenty of gourmet-style catering for friends, colleagues and clients for some time, albeit privately at home, and had been a closet chef for years, but this was something completely different. Relatively speaking, this was the big leagues.

Essentially we were faced with a decision that would change our lives completely: We had to either sell up everything and move lock, stock and barrel to the Karoo and go into a whole new life as complete novices, or forget the whole thing and carry on as we were, risking our family unit and life as we knew it.

In hindsight, I suppose the decision was simple.

Within four months we had packed up our home and moved to our beloved Karoo town and new home of Graaff-Reinet. On 1 April 2008 (April Fool's Day) Rose took over the guesthouse while I finished up my responsibilities in the corporate world and sorted out things in Port Elizabeth. Two months later I moved up to take over the kitchen and help run the newly acquired business.

And so, with no formal training, no experience and no help from the previous owners, we had begun to realise

our impossible dream. To top it off, we managed to time it all to coincide perfectly with the start of the greatest global recession since the 1930s! Fortunately, I did have a few good things going for me. A massively supportive wife (and business partner), two fantastic boys who I could now see every day, the sort of genuine friends and community support that one can only get in the Karoo, access to fantastic fresh ingredients through my relationships with my old school friends who farmed in the area and, lastly and possibly most importantly, an obsession with good Karoo food.

As we progressed through a shaky start, I began to spread my wings and back myself in the kitchen. I began focusing on my strengths and my residual knowledge of the kitchen and food, instead of trying to emulate those who had gone before me. The restaurant had a massive reputation and I thought I had some big shoes to fill. After bumping my head more than a few times, I realised that I also had a pair of my own shoes and I had a hell of a lot more confidence in them. Funnily enough, the more I wore them, the more comfy they got. I also realised that there was a big gap in the market for top-end authentic Karoo-style cooking, just my forte.

Gordon's Restaurant started gaining a reputation for good, honest Karoo food and, as importantly, I was really starting to have some fun. After I joined the Slow Food movement (www.slowfood.com) and was asked to start a Karoo convivium (branch), I was invited to their international convention in Turin, Italy in 2010.

I was so inspired by what was going on and how similar their ideas and ethos were to mine, that the idea of *Veld to Fork* – the book – was born. The time had come for me to take off my apron (temporarily, of course) and put pen to paper.

With regard to what happens further on in this book, please let's be very clear on one major point: I am not a qualified chef, nor do I have any formal training as one. I am just a good ol' country boy at heart with a deep-seated passion for the Karoo, its people and its food.

You will note that there are very few complicated recipes in this book as I hope to show you that with simple, quality ingredients, some time and a good dollop of enthusiasm, anyone can cook.

This is the story of a Karoo lover's food journey and what I have learned so far …

The Karoo, Graaff-Reinet and its people

To me, the Karoo is the heart and soul of South Africa. A hard, hostile-looking place on the surface, beneath this thin veneer lies the true spirit of our beloved country, full of diverse people all co-existing in a simple yet beautifully dynamic blend of cultures. This union, forged together through centuries of hardship and pain, has resulted in an unbelievably rich and generous spirit of kinship towards one's fellow man, which shines through in the legendary hospitality and humanity of all its people. The Karoo is truly a place that is good for the soul.

THE HISTORY

Graaff-Reinet, where I live, is the oldest town in the Eastern Cape and the fourth oldest in South Africa. During the seventeenth and eighteenth centuries Dutch burghers (citizens) began to leave the Cape to escape the oppression of the Dutch administrative government. These burghers became known as *trek boers* and were noted for their hardy, independent character, disdain for authority and dislike of taxes.

To keep some control over their subjects, the Dutch authorities established, in 1786, a *drostdy* (an administrative centre) in a picturesque setting where the Sundays River flows from the Sneeuberg mountains. They named the settlement after the then Governor of the Cape colony, Cornelis Jacob van de Graaff, and his wife, whose maiden name was Reynet.

One of the first Landdrosts (chief magistrates) was a young man by the name of (Sir) Andries Stockenström. He became a prominent figure in the history of the town and district. His home is the site of our guesthouse, a lovely old manor house (c. 1819) in the heart of the old Graaff-Reinet.

Eve Palmer, in her literary classic *The Plains of Camdeboo*, describes early Graaff-Reinet thus:

When the first travelers ventured here at the end of the 18th century … Graaff Reinet was a little village with a half dozen houses built of mud where it was difficult to remain in a lighted room by night for the bats that came out of the thatched roofs by the thousand and blew out the candles with the wind they caused.

Twenty years later it was the most picturesque town in the Cape, an oasis on the river, with flat roofed, white washed houses and wide streets planted with orange and lemon trees, vines, oleanders, pomegranates and great quince hedges bent down with fruit.

It hummed with life. There was a church, school, court of law, a smith, wagon maker, shops and traders in ostrich hides, soap and butter.

In the 1830s there was a mass movement of boers away from the Colony to the North, where they hoped to establish republics where they would be independent. This was the Great Trek, which had huge ramifications for the history of South Africa. The majority of those on the Trek came from the Eastern Cape. Andries Pretorius, a Graaff-Reinet farmer, left from his farm Letskraal and became one of the Great Trek's most famous leaders. He commanded the Boers at the Battle of Blood River and later became the first president of the South African Republic. Pretoria was named after him.

Graaff-Reinet has one of the most attractive settings of any town in South Africa: mountains on three sides and the flat plains of the Camdeboo to the south. Few places have conserved their townscape as well as Graaff-Reinet and the town has more protected buildings than any other in South Africa. The most prominent of these is the Dutch Reformed Church (*see pic on page 15*), which is a Victorian Gothic gem. Another notable structure is the Old Drostdy, as well as several splendid examples of Cape Dutch and unique Karoo Dutch architecture, such as Reinet House, Urquhart House and the old Residency.

Since the days of the 'Graaff-Reinet Republic', the town has always been in the forefront of historical processes in South Africa. During the guerilla phase of the Anglo-Boer War, raiders from the Transvaal and Free State operated widely in the rugged terrain of the area, supported by much of the Afrikaans populace. Many, although subjects

of the Queen, took up arms and joined the Boers, becoming known as Cape Rebels.

As the centre of British military operations for the Eastern Cape, a large garrison of the Coldstream Guards was stationed in Graaff-Reinet to try to quell the situation. They commandeered the Graaff-Reinet Club (*see pic on left*) as their officer's mess and today there are still bullet holes in the bar counter as reminders of their drunken escapades. Many of the Cape Rebels were taken prisoner and charged with high treason. A number were shot by firing squad, the most controversial being Gideon Scheepers, a Boer commander who was executed outside the town. When the Van Ryneveld's Pass (now Ngweba) Dam was built, his grave was covered by the resultant lake.

FAMOUS FOLK FROM GRAAFF-REINET

The names of famous Graaff-Reinetters and those from its surrounds reads like the who's who of South African history, some more infamous than famous and some downright quirky. The first of these must have been Chief Hykon-Koebaha or Lord of all the Inqua Tribe. In about 1689 he was reputed to be the leader of the richest Khoikhoi (as they were then known) tribe in southern Africa.

Then there was Koerikei, a San leader who rebelled against the Dutch farmers and famously shouted from the top of a cliff to his pursuers: 'You have taken all the places where the eland lived. Why do you not go back to where you came from; there where the sun sets?'

Adriaan van Jaarsveld was a Commandant of the Boers in the district and later instigator of the Graaff-Reinet Republic of 1795. He is reputed to be the first Graaff-Reinet citizen to die in the jail at the Castle in Cape Town.

World-renowned botanist Harry Bolus, founder of the Bolus Herbarium, lived here, as did Andrew Geddes Bain, esteemed geologist, road engineer, palaeontologist and explorer. During the 13 years he lived here, however, he worked as a humble saddle maker. He helped with the construction of the Ouberg Pass and supervised the construction of the Van Ryneveld's Pass. In 1837 he was appointed superintendent of military roads by the Royal Engineers. He built eight mountain passes, including Mitchell's Pass and Bain's Kloof Pass. He can also rightly be called the father of South African palaeontology. His first fossil discovery was made in 1838. He is also famous for a fossil he discovered with a very impressive jaw filled with teeth, which he named the 'Blinkwater Monster'. His second son and seventh child, Thomas (Bain), became an even more famous road builder than his father and is the best known of the nineteenth-century road builders.

Sticking with palaeontology, Dr Sidney Rubidge was a farmer on Wellwood farm in the district. His hobby of fossil collecting became so highly developed that it brought him worldwide recognition for his contribution to science in the field of palaeontology. He built and maintained a fossil museum on Wellwood, which has come to be recognised as the finest private collection of Karoo fossils in the world.

Prof. James Kitching (family of my great mate Shaun – see the Eland Steak Roll recipe on page 93), who grew up in the district, was a South African vertebrate palaeontologist and is regarded as one of the world's greatest fossil finders.

William Smith is South Africa's best-known and most popular television science and mathematics teacher. As with many of our famous townsfolk, he matriculated at the Union High School at the end of Caledon Street. A few years ago he was voted 86th in the Top 100 Great South Africans. The first coelacanth, or 'living fossil', was discovered by Smith's father, Prof. James LB Smith, a renowned ichthyologist.

Business tycoon, philanthropist and environmentalist Dr Anton Rupert was born here, and his family still farm in the district. Robert Sobukwe, one of South Africa's most famous anti-apartheid activists and best known for founding the Pan African Congress, was born and is buried here.

Arthur Short, born and still farming in the Graaff-Reinet district with his sons David and Lloyd, was an awesome opening batsman. He was twice selected as a Springbok cricketer, being named in the 1970 squad to tour England and also selected, together with his neighbour 'Dassie' Biggs, for the 1971–72 tour to Australia. Unfortunately both trips were cancelled. Many in the know reckon he could have been one of the all-time greats. The Wheatlands Sports Club is situated on their farm and both of his boys are still active cricketers there.

Two rather infamous and colourful ladies with origins in the town are Sophia Werner and Sylvia Raphael. Sophia, better known as Black Sophie because of her dark complexion, was born in Graaff-Reinet in 1827. She became a well-known madam of a brothel in Bree Street, Cape Town. Sylvia was a Graaff-Reinet-born Christian with a Jewish father, and she became one of the leading female operatives in Mossad, Israel's external intelligence agency. Posing as a Canadian photojournalist under the alias Patricia Roxborough, she was one of the first Mossad agents to penetrate Yasser Arafat's bases in Jordan and Lebanon in the 1960s. She was also reputed to be closely involved in Israel's partially successful attempts to track down the PLO terrorists responsible for the deaths of 11 Israeli athletes at the 1972 Munich Olympics.

Closer to my time at Union High School, I had many 'soon to be famous' friends and acquaintances, amongst them Sonia Doubell, now a London-based actress, model and singer who found fame as a Bond girl, starring alongside Pierce Brosnan in the film *Die Another Day*. Isobel Dixon is the author of two books and won the unpublished section of the Sanlam Prize in South Africa in 2000 and the Olive Schreiner Prize in 2004.

The list goes on and on and who knows, maybe I will crack a nod on it one day too.

THE PEOPLE AND SURROUNDS

Graaff-Reinet is almost completely surrounded by the Camdeboo National Park, which includes the well-known Valley of Desolation, a dramatic cleft in the ironstone rocks. The town is also the centre of a sheep farming area well known for the quality of its wool and mutton, and we all know that Karoo lamb is the finest in the world. The Angora goat is farmed here in great numbers too, and our little town is thus regarded as the mohair capital of the world.

There is, however, one thing that truly differentiates Graaff-Reinet, and indeed the Karoo, from other parts of the world. Its people. Despite the harshness of the climate and life in the Karoo (or possibly because of it) there is humility, friendliness and a sense of kinship amongst those born of the Karoo that is hard to find anywhere else. The saying out here goes: 'Never be rude to your neighbour, you never know when you will need him next.' If only this was a universal ethic …

One of the first things visitors to the Karoo comment on is its people, their friendliness, candour and humility. The hospitality of the people of the Karoo is legendary and the town of Graaff-Reinet, fondly referred to as the 'Gem of the Karoo', is no exception. We have so many wonderful friends, places and pastimes in our community and I shall endeavour to introduce you to a few of them and share some of their recipes with you in this book. I hope you become as fond of them as I am.

Soups

Soups make for a wonderfully nourishing meal-in-one. What could be better on a cold Karoo winter's evening than sitting around the fire with a hearty bowl of soup, some thick, crusty bread and a glass of sherry? Mmm …

Seven-bean classic Karoo boontjiesop – my style

Boontjiesop (bean soup) is one of the ultimate and most traditional winter soups in the Karoo. It's full of protein power and goodness. It also freezes superbly so is great to make in one big batch at the start of winter and then freeze in smaller containers to take out and reheat on those cold wintery evenings.

You can make this as a vegetarian or meaty soup. If, like me, you like a bit of meat, go with the full recipe as given below. For a vegetarian version, just leave out the meat and use vegetable instead of chicken stock. The nice thing about this recipe is that it is really easy to chop and change so you can add whatever extras you fancy or leave out bits you don't.

This is the full monty version that I use in the restaurant so you may not have access to all the ingredients (such as Parma ham bones), but feel free to experiment with your own version and add or substitute ingredients from what you have available. The key here is to have a good base stock, good-quality beans and a Sunday afternoon to spare, as this baby does not like to be rushed. This is comfort food in the first degree.

---

3 litres water

1 litre chicken or vegetable stock

100 g each dried haricot beans, sugar beans, butter beans, kidney beans, jugo beans (African groundnuts), cow peas and black beans (or any combination of good dried beans you fancy), soaked overnight

250 g soup mix (at most supermarkets; it's essentially a combination of dried lentils, split peas, barley, etc.)

300 g pork trotters (ask your butcher to cut them into pieces for you – these add natural gelatine for thickening and, of course, buckets of flavour)

6 cloves garlic, peeled

5 stalks celery, roughly chopped

1 kg venison meaty bones (beef or lamb shank will also work)

250 g roughly chopped bacon (I use my own Parma-style ham bits here)

500 g marrow bones or Parma ham bone (the Parma bone adds wonderful flavour)

1 handful each fresh rosemary and oregano

15 ml mild curry powder

1 large aubergine, peeled and chopped (this will help thicken the soup but be sure not to let it stand before adding to the pot as it tends to go brown if you leave it exposed to air)

Salt and freshly ground pepper

Fill a large saucepan with the water and stock. Add the rest of the ingredients. Ensure that everything is well covered; if not, top up with more water. Bring to the boil.

Once boiling nicely, reduce the heat and simmer for at least 3 hours, stirring occasionally, until the meat is falling off the bones and the beans are soft. Remove all the meaty bits/bones and place them to one side to cool.

Once cooled, cut off all the meat from the bones, remove the marrow and chop up into small pieces. Return the meat to the pot and give the bones to your dog.

Give the soup a good stir, taste, add salt and pepper as necessary and you are good to go.

Serve with hot crusty bread, a good grind of black pepper and a nice sherry at the fireside.

SERVES 10–12

Curried sweet potato and parsnip soup

I love sweet potatoes and my mom re-introduced me to the long forgotten but wonderful parsnip a few years back. I managed to get some seed and have been growing them ever since. They are very versatile and look like an overgrown white carrot. Much like a sweet potato, parsnips also turn brown when peeled and exposed to air so make sure you keep them submerged in water or chop them straight into the pot when using them.

This soup is spiced just enough to make sure all your taste buds are singing hymns by the second spoonful, but not so much as to burn the cr*p out of you. Aaah, heaven in a bowl …

---

30 ml olive oil

1 onion, diced

2 cloves garlic, minced

45 ml curry powder

3 sweet potatoes, peeled and cut into 5 cm chunks

5 parsnips, peeled and roughly chopped

5 ml white pepper, or to taste

5 ml cayenne pepper or chilli powder

5 ml salt, or to taste

1 litre vegetable stock, or enough to cover

Wonder salt (see page 151)

Heat the olive oil in a large stock pot over medium heat. Add the onion, garlic and curry powder. Sweat off lightly until the onion starts to turn translucent.

Add the sweet potatoes, parsnips, white pepper, cayenne pepper and salt. Cover with stock and stir to combine.

Bring to the boil, then reduce to a simmer and cook for 20 minutes. Taste the broth and add salt to taste, if necessary. Simmer until the sweet potatoes and parsnips are soft and mash easily with a fork.

When cooked, blend with a stick blender, give it a stir and add a pinch or two of wonder salt to taste.

Serve with toasted pumpkin seeds, a dash of fresh cream and some chopped walnuts fried in a knob of butter.

SERVES 5–7

Carrot soup with orange and ginger

This is a great rejuvenating and healthy soup, ideal as a starter or a light meal. If you are feeling like you are coming down with the flu or are already in the throes of it, whip up a batch and just the sight of it will make you feel better. The orange is full of vitamin C and ginger has long been used as a remedy for colds and flu, and it has a very positive effect on the digestive tract. The carrots are chock-full of beta-carotene and vitamin A, which helps the liver flush out toxins, so it's good for a hangover too. If you are not unwell, have some anyway to help your body stay healthy. It also freezes really well for that quick rainy or anyday snack.

---

500 g carrots, roughly chopped
250 ml chicken stock
15 ml chopped fresh ginger
5 ml ground ginger
10 ml cumin seeds
250 ml fresh orange juice
15 ml butter
250 ml fresh or sour cream
4 chives, snipped
Zest of ½ orange

Place the carrots and stock in a saucepan and cook until soft. Place the carrots and stock in a blender with the fresh and ground ginger, and the cumin seeds. Blend until smooth.

Add the orange juice and butter and blend again.

Return the soup to the saucepan and reheat (do not boil). Serve with a dollop of cream, some snipped chives and orange zest.

SERVES 4–6

Elsanne's beetroot, onion and garlic soup

I got this recipe from my crazy mate Elsanne McNaughton, who farms with her husband Adrian (Adie) on their farm Houtconstant in the Graaff-Reinet district. Together with Adie's brother Ronald and his wife Sandy, their Charmac Stud is famous for its top-quality Geelbek Merino sheep.

Elsanne also runs a B&B on the farm (http://www.hgfarm.co.za) and is a very keen cook. Her guests never go hungry thanks to the traditional farm fare she produces right off the land and we often swap recipes.

This old family recipe of hers is such an earthy soup (each main ingredient comes from under the ground) and is wonderful and hearty. Even though the three main ingredients have strong individual flavours, they come together to form a superb ménage à trois *with no single ingredient overpowering the other. Just don't get any on your clothes!*

4 beetroot, wrapped in aluminium foil and baked at 180 °C for 1 hour, or until soft
4 large onions, sliced
16 cloves garlic, peeled
1 litre chicken stock
Salt and freshly ground pepper
Zest of 1 lemon
250 ml fresh cream
2 ml turmeric (borrie)
5 ml curry powder
50 ml grated fresh horseradish or 60 ml horseradish cream

Peel and slice the cooked beetroot. Combine the beetroot, onions, garlic and stock, and bring to the boil. Reduce the heat and simmer until the liquid has reduced by half. Liquidise or force through a sieve and season with salt and pepper to taste.

Ladle the soup into bowls and add zest to each bowl.

Whip the cream, turmeric and curry powder until stiff, and then fold in the horseradish. Divide the mixture among the soup bowls and serve.

SERVES 4–6

Blue cheese, biltong and port soup

This robust winter's soup absolutely needs four to six friends and a nice log fire as your primary ingredients. I use whatever biltong I have available, but springbok remains my favourite. Your butcher should be able to help you with biltong shavings if you don't have any.

My mate Arno Bouwer and his wife Tracy just love this soup and are always asking me to make it. We met them when we first moved to Graaff-Reinet and they have become great friends. Turns out Arno and I were at university together in Port Elizabeth, even though we never knew each other at the time. It's crazy how life moves in circles.

65 g butter
125 ml cake flour
10 ml freshly ground black pepper
2 ml freshly ground coriander
2 ml grated nutmeg
250 ml milk
750 ml good-quality chicken stock
125 ml grated Cheddar cheese
150 g finely grated moist biltong
100 ml fresh cream
50 g blue cheese
150 ml port

Melt the butter in a heavy-based saucepan and add the cake flour and spices. Heat slowly and stir continuously. Remove from the heat once the mixture is smooth and creamy, approximately 5 minutes.

Mix the milk and stock together and gradually add to the butter and flour mixture. Return to moderate heat and whisk continuously until it thickens.

Remove from the heat and add the Cheddar cheese and half of the biltong. Return to low heat and simmer for 5 minutes. Do not allow the mixture to boil again.

Add the cream, blue cheese and port just before serving. Garnish with a dash of cream and the remaining biltong.

SERVES 6–8

Meat

I love working with meat, from selecting the animal on the farm or hunting it myself, to hanging and working the meat and preparing it all the way through to the final tasty morsel on my plate.

For me it is imperative to know where the meat came from and how the animal was treated. Its life should be healthy and generally without stress, it should have been fed good-quality food, and ideally reared and raised on the veld.

With game it is even more important to look after the meat from the very first point of contact. When game is hunted incorrectly it suffers stress and adrenaline is released and eventually lactic acid. This gives the meat a 'gamey' flavour. In my opinion, if you can taste gaminess in your venison, it was poorly hunted. You can read more about this on page 83.

I am not keen on so-called 'grain-fed' meat products as, in reality, this is just mass produced, hormone-fuelled feedlot production with very little consideration given to the welfare of the animals or the consumer. Veld-reared is almost always better for both the animal and you.

I like to carve the meat at the table when I am entertaining at home. In the restaurant, however, this is not possible and one learns quickly the value of letting a freshly cooked cut of meat rest before carving or slicing. If you don't, you end up with the tasty juices on the serving platter and not in the meat. Resting allows those precious juices to settle and be reabsorbed into the meat fibres, ensuring a tender, juicy cut. You also then have time to make the gravy and have a glass of wine.

Hanging/ripening/ageing meat is also important. As meat ripens, the fibres are exposed to oxygen and start to break down. This tenderises the cut naturally. Meat is often vacuum sealed, which helps to preserve it for longer in an oxygen-free environment. This works great, but when you open the packet you often get a grey-looking piece of meat with a funky smell, making some people think that the meat is turning or off. If you take the meat out of the packaging and place it in a marinating dish in the fridge for a while, it will get all its colour back and will look and smell great. Vacuum sealing is, unfortunately, also open to abuse and blood and water may be included in the bag so you end up paying for liquid that ruins the meat and gets poured down the sink. Check cuts carefully before buying.

Most meat purchased from a large butcher or supermarket is not properly aged (unless specifically stated) because ageing meat costs money. Buy from a reputable dealer, or ripen the meat at home yourself. A nice rump steak out of its packaging and placed in a suitable container will ripen in the fridge in a few days. Be sure to turn it every day to keep it from drying out. If you fancy a steak on Friday, put it in the fridge on Monday. You won't believe the difference in taste and tenderness.

In the Karoo the staple red meats are lamb, venison and beef. Chicken and pork are considered 'vegetarian' options and fresh fish is a delicacy you only have on holiday at the coast or when your relatives come up to visit from the Cape and bring you a nice smoked snoek.

Karoo Lamb and Mutton

Lamb is the *crème de la crème* of meats from the Karoo and people visit from all over the world to taste it.

I love cooking lamb, from shanks and stews to roasts with whole cloves of garlic pressed into the flesh. They say the nicest meat is closest to the bone, an ethos I wholly subscribe to, and a Karoo lamb neck slow-roasted in the oven or in a kettle braai is such a treat. Sticky lamb ribs are an all-time hit too and no holiday trip would be complete without a lamb and mint pie as *padkos* (food for the journey).

But first let's clear up a few misconceptions regarding lamb. You will note that the heading of this chapter refers to lamb *and* mutton. Although people tend to refer to both as lamb, there is quite a big difference.

In the Karoo, lamb tends to be exactly that: a young sheep roughly 1 year old with less than two teeth (*twee tand* as they say locally) and weighing around 40 kg (live weight). It is graded A or AB, with a classification number of 1 to 6 (with 1 being very thin and miserable, and 6 being really fatty). I use grade AB 2 or 3, which I consider the best grade lamb, as it comes from a young, fairly well developed animal with a 4–5 mm layer of fat and good meat to bone ratio, i.e. not too much bone and good meat coverage.

Mutton comes from an animal older than 1 year, that is larger than a lamb and more developed, and has 2 to 6 teeth. It falls into the B and C categories and is classed from 2 to 3. A good quality buy for mutton would be graded, for example, B 2.

Whilst lamb tends to be much tenderer than mutton and is used by restaurateurs for their prime cuts, mutton has way more flavour but generally needs a longer cooking time. Either way it's a compromise between tenderness

and flavour, so think about what you want to do with the cut before deciding what to buy. A tender chop on the braai (barbecue) should be lamb, but mutton is the best choice for a tasty winter casserole or stew. When in doubt, ask your butcher.

I recommend you find a local butcher who is approachable and helpful and build a good relationship with him or her so that you get decent advice while at the same time supporting a local neighborhood business.

Now that you know what to look for when buying lamb, you need to know what makes Karoo lamb so special. The not so big secret about Karoo lamb and mutton is that it is raised and lives entirely out in the veld. It very seldom has any form of supplementary feeding, unlike most other livestock, and the old adage of 'you are what you eat' rings absolutely true.

The Karoo is situated in an arid semi-desert region which, at first glance and to the untrained eye, looks like nothing much at all. In reality, however, it is a massively rich and diverse environment that has developed over millions of years and is teeming with life.

The veld itself is a rich array of shrubs, grasses, succulents and wild herbs, including wild rosemary, camphor, lavender and sage. Essentially, what all these plants have in common are high concentrations of terpenoids and other volatile oils. Plant terpenoids are used extensively for their aromatic qualities and in traditional herbal remedies. This unique combination gives Karoo lamb and mutton its delicate flavour and makes it every cook's dream to work with, as very little needs to be done in order to bring out the best flavour. I'm sure the recipes that follow will testify to this.

Minty mutton summer stew

Lamb and mint is a famous combination, so why not try a fresh and minty mutton stew, just right for a summer's evening.

2 onions, chopped
6 cloves garlic
3 sprigs fresh thyme, chopped
Olive oil
500 g mutton neck, cut into pieces
500 g mutton flank, cubed
Salt and freshly ground pepper
4 tomatoes, peeled and chopped
1 stalk celery, chopped
2 carrots, roughly chopped
8 baby potatoes
1 aubergine, chopped
250 ml water or stock
5 golden patty pans
1 handful chopped fresh mint
1 handful fresh spinach
5 florets broccoli

Fry the onions, garlic and thyme in a glug of olive oil in a stovetop-to-oven casserole dish until browned. Remove from the dish and set aside.

Brown the meat in batches, adding seasoning as you go. Return all the meat and the onion mixture to the casserole. Add the tomatoes, celery, carrots, potatoes, aubergine and water. Cover with the lid and simmer for 1 hour.

Add the patty pans and simmer for 5 minutes, then gently stir in the mint, spinach and broccoli and allow to simmer for another 15 minutes.

A glass or two of good Shiraz will work well with this dish.

SERVES 4–6

Rustic braised lamb shanks with beans

A recipe sure to steal a farmer's heart. My old school bud Jean de la Harpe lives on the picturesque farm Grassdale in the Sneeuberg mountains, northwest of Graaff-Reinet. We have been mates for what seems an eternity and Jean's Dohne Merino stud (named Normandy Stud, after the province on the coast of France where his family originates) is one of the finest in southern Africa. His family has been farming in the region for generations and he is a true son of the Karoo. Although he is a bit of a legend with the ladies, he seems determined to remain the eternal bachelor. (Rose, however, is convinced that one day she will find him a wife.)

Jean has some of the best lamb around, with a very subtle and delicate flavour that is only achievable in the mountains with their sneeubossies and lush summer grasses. He was so spoilt with his beautiful lamb that he used to consider lamb shanks only good for dog food. That was until Rose and I showed him the error of his ways and how to cook them properly. Long and slow is the only way … So if you're looking to land a handsome farmer or just feel like a romantic evening around the fire with a loved one, here is a route straight to their heart – easy, tasty and with lots of slow cooking to ensure plenty of time for romance.

Olive oil
1 onion, chopped
2 lamb shanks
Salt and freshly ground pepper
1 can (400 g) baked beans in tomato sauce
4 glasses good red wine
2 carrots, chopped
6 cloves garlic (garlic is an aphrodisiac – trust me …)
1 stalk celery, chopped
1 handful fresh rosemary

Preheat the oven to 160 °C.

Heat a good glug of olive oil in a heavy-based stovetop-to-oven casserole, and fry the onion until soft.

Add the shanks and brown them, adding salt and pepper to taste. When browned, add the beans, 2 glasses of the wine and the remaining ingredients. Cover with the lid and place in the oven for 2 hours, or until the meat is soft and falling off the bone. (If the meat is still tough, don't panic, just make sure there is enough liquid in the pot, put the lid back on and cook for longer until the meat gets really tender.)

Once soft, remove the lid and continue baking for about 20 minutes. While you wait, pour the remaining 2 glasses of wine for yourself and your dinner partner and sip them by the fire while you wait for the meat to brown with the lid removed (additional wine may well be necessary).

The beans will cook away, forming a lovely thick sauce with the red wine, and the meat should be succulent and falling off the bone when ready.

Serve on top of buttery mash with a good few spoons of the thick sauce and another glass of red wine.

If you do this correctly, you should be well on your way to acquiring a new spouse or, at worst, you will have had a lovely evening with your new best friend. Good luck!

SERVES 2

Classic roast leg of mutton

There is something iconic about a Sunday roast in the Karoo. If you ever end up having lunch on a Sunday in the Karoo, there is a really good chance that there will be a delicious roast hiding in an oven somewhere. The aromas are unmistakable and I can think of no better way to spend a meal than with friends and family and a nice big mutton roast. Remember that mutton has much more flavour than lamb but requires a bit more cooking to ensure it is beautifully tender.

My favourite way of roasting a leg – sticky, smoky and sweet – is on a braai. I use my kettle braai but you can also do it in the oven at 180 °C.

1 mutton roast (2.5–3.5 kg), shank still attached
125 ml chopped fresh rosemary
60 ml chopped fresh ginger
125 ml chopped garlic
1 handful cracked black pepper
1 handful sea salt flakes
15 ml mustard powder
125 ml apricot jam
Olive oil

Using a sharp knife, score the fat on the roast in a diamond pattern to help release the fat during roasting. Make a paste with the remaining ingredients and rub it all over the meat. Set aside for 1 hour for this deliciously sticky rub to draw in.

Place the leg on a big roasting tray and roast in the heated kettle braai over indirect coals (30 briquettes on each side) for 2½–3 hours, or until the meat is well done and pulling off the bone.

Remove from the kettle braai and rest for 20 minutes before carving. Serve with magic potatoes (see page 128), gravy (see page 58) and crisp vegetables.

SERVES 6–8

Sticky ribs on the braai

Ribs are always such a treat and make the best finger food. The way I like them is slow-cooked (surprise!) on the braai with a sticky sauce. If you rush a rib it will be tough; nice and slow over a very moderate heat and you will have the juiciest and tenderest ribs imaginable. The moderate heat will also ensure the sticky sauce does not burn.

30 ml runny honey
15 ml olive oil
15 ml soy sauce
1 sprig finely chopped fresh rosemary
1 rack lamb or mutton ribs

Mix the honey, oil, soy sauce and rosemary together and brush over the ribs generously. Marinate overnight.

Take the ribs out in time to return to room temperature before braaiing. When the coals are ready (remember, a nice moderate heat), place the ribs in a clamp grid and braai slowly, basting and turning often. They should take at least 45–60 minutes. Don't rush them and keep the heat nice and low and they will turn out beautifully.

When done, remove from the grid, allow to cool slightly and cut them into sections. Eat using your fingers. Mmm … sticky and sweet!

SERVES 4

Roasted lamb neck with fresh rosemary

Neck is a tough cut so it needs to be cooked long and slow to allow the meat to soften. It is, however, unbelievably full of flavour and makes a lovely soft roast when cooked correctly. You will note that I have added salty anchovy fillets to the recipe. I know it sounds crazy but, trust me, it works. The little fishy fillets melt away, yet they lift the dish to a whole new level and bring out the flavour of the lamb. You also need to start with a very hot oven, to seal the meat nicely, then slow it right down. As I said, trust me … you'll love it.

1 whole lamb neck
6 cloves garlic, halved
4 whole anchovy fillets (the ones you buy in the little bottle that are pickled and brined), chopped
Olive oil
Salt and freshly ground pepper
250 ml chicken stock
250 ml white wine
1 handful fresh rosemary sprigs

Preheat the oven to it's hottest setting (280 °C if your oven goes that high).

There is a thick white strip of connective tissue that runs the full length of the neck. Before seasoning the roast, take a sharp knife and cut along the sides of this white strip, from top to bottom, then cut it a few times crossways. If you don't do this it tends to curl up during the cooking process and the roast will be difficult to carve.

Make small incisions in the neck and stuff alternately with garlic and anchovy fillets. Rub the whole neck with oil, season with salt and pepper, and place in a casserole dish.

Add the chicken stock, wine and rosemary. Place into the oven for 10 minutes with the lid off. Reduce the oven temperature to 160 °C, put the lid on the dish and roast slowly for 2½–3 hours, or until the meat is soft and tender and falling off the bone. Make sure that there is enough liquid in the casserole dish at all times.

Remove the lid and increase the oven temperature to 200 °C for 15 minutes to brown the meat.

Remove from the oven and set aside to rest. You should have lots of lovely pan juices for gravy (see page 58).

To carve the neck, slice along the length of the roast from top to bottom and use the carving fork to pull the meat from the bone.

SERVES 6

KAROO LAMB AND MUTTON 37

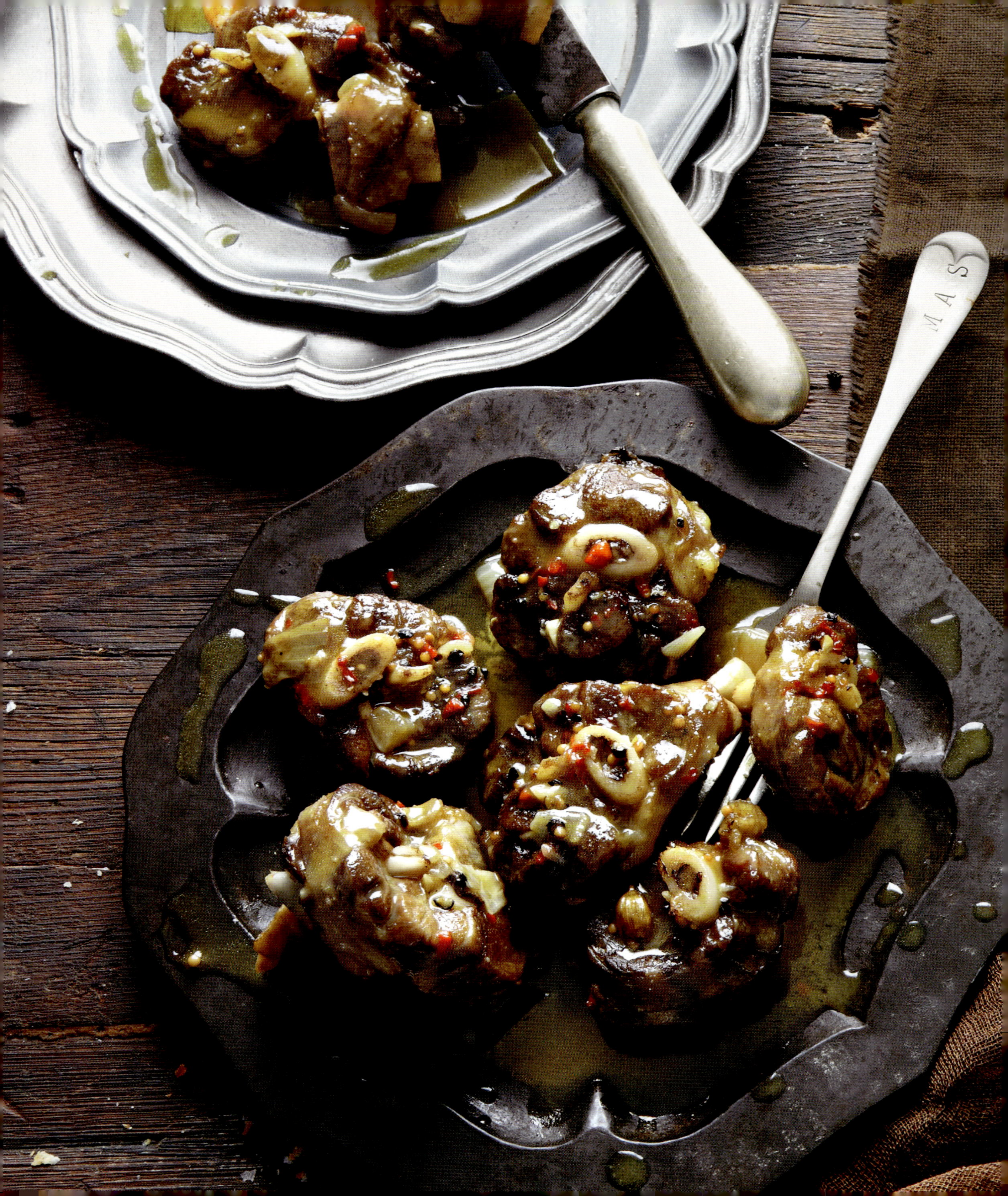
MAS

Spicy mutton knuckles with garlic parsnip mash

This is a really tasty and hearty dish that is boosted by the parsnip mash. It's great for winter or whenever you need a cosy night in with some mates around the fire, a decent bottle of wine and a good old chat.

1 red onion, chopped
3 cloves garlic, finely chopped
2 thumb-sized pieces fresh ginger, finely chopped
3 chillies, chopped (seeds removed if you don't want too much heat)
2 cardamom pods, cracked
5 ml turmeric
10 ml mustard seeds
Olive oil
1 kg mutton knuckles
250 ml chicken stock
1 handful fresh coriander
Salt and freshly ground pepper

GARLIC PARSNIP MASH
8 parsnips, peeled and chopped
1 whole bulb garlic
Knob of butter
Salt and freshly ground pepper
Paprika

To make the mutton stew, sweat off the onion, garlic, ginger, chillies and spices in a good glug of olive oil in a heavy-based saucepan, then remove from the pan and set aside. Using the same pan, brown the meat in batches. Return all the meat and the onion mixture to the saucepan and add the stock. Simmer for 45–60 minutes.

To make the mash, place the parsnips and whole garlic into a saucepan of salted water (enough to cover) and boil for 30 minutes until soft. Remove, drain and allow to steam dry. Once cool enough to handle, squeeze the garlic out of the cloves onto the parsnips, add the butter, season to taste and mash until smooth. Scoop the mash into an ovenproof dish, sprinkle with some paprika and add a few more dabs of butter, and place under a preheated oven grill until the top is golden.

When the meat is nice and soft, stir in the coriander, season to taste and you are good to go. Serve the mutton knuckles on top of the mash and add a sprinkling of fresh coriander.

SERVES 2–4

Black pepper lamb casserole

Black pepper is one of the world's favourite spices and is found in almost all cuisines across the globe. I love its spicy flavour and how it brings out a unique flavour in lamb that I really enjoy. I came across a similar recipe through my slow food connections and have tweaked it slightly to suit our lovely Karoo lamb. This is a relatively easy dish and should not take too long to prep and cook (about 1½ hours). Enjoy with a bold Cabernet Sauvignon or Pinotage.

Olive oil
1 small onion, finely chopped
10 black peppercorns, whole or ground
700 g lamb, cubed (ideally from a leg roast)
4 medium tomatoes, peeled and chopped
5 whole cloves garlic
1 aubergine, peeled and cubed
2 carrots, peeled and finely diced
2 small potatoes, peeled and cubed
Salt

Heat the oil in a deep frying pan and sauté the onion and peppercorns. Add the lamb and sauté until browned. Add the tomatoes, garlic, aubergine and two spoonfuls of water. Cook and simmer over low heat for 40 minutes.

Add the carrots and potatoes and continue cooking for 20 minutes. Add salt to taste.

Serve hot with warm crusty bread to mop up the sauce.

SERVES 4

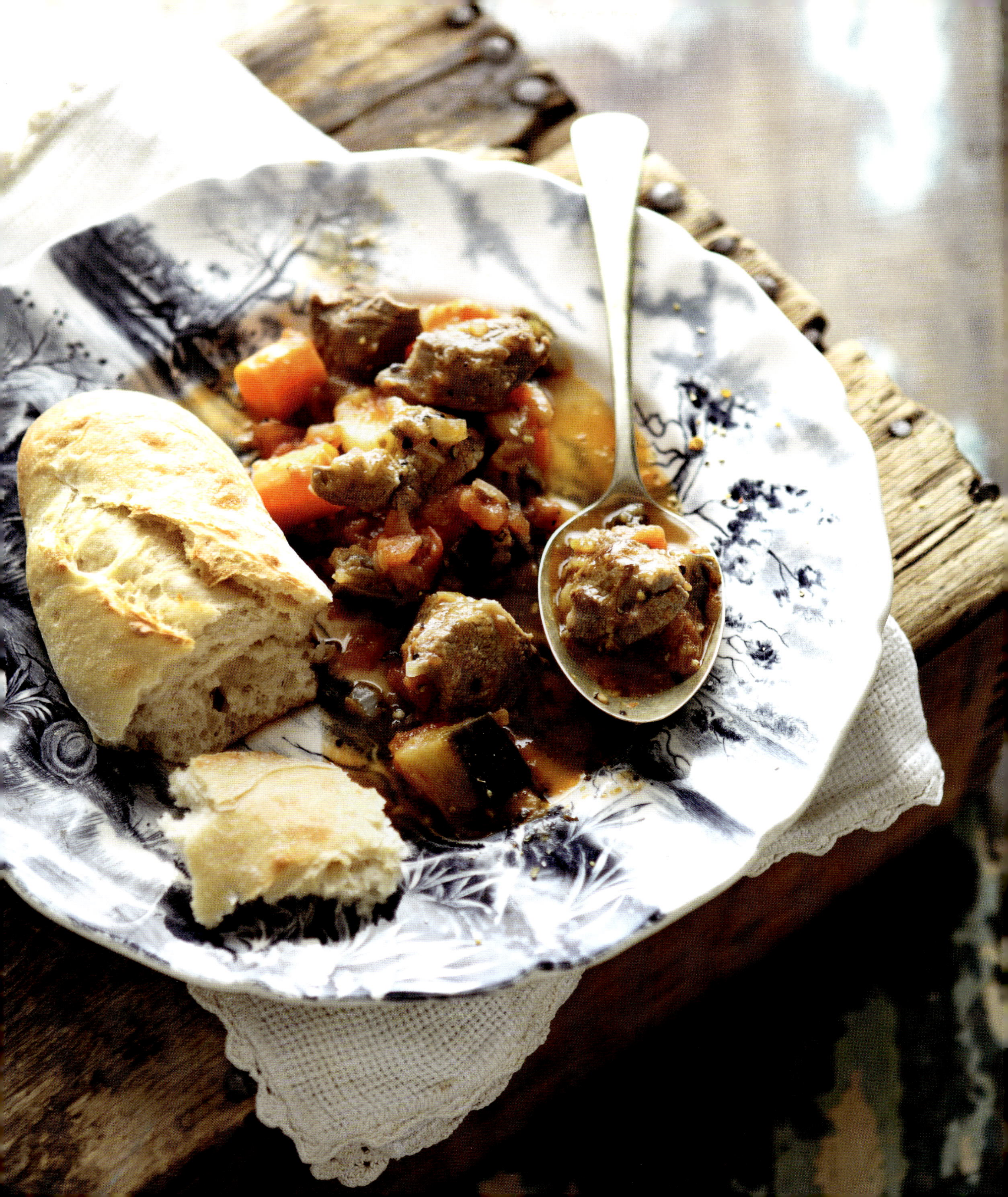

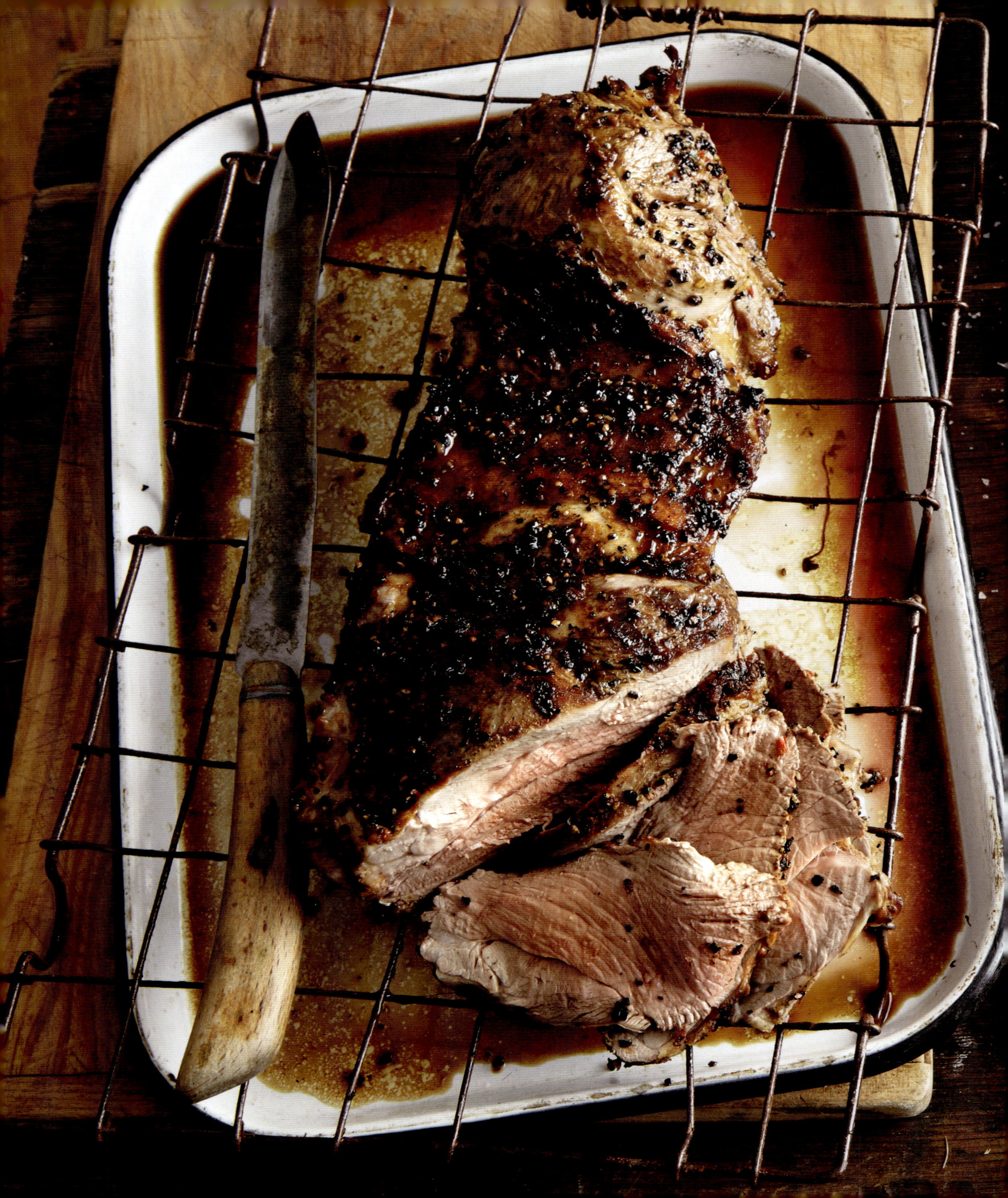

Chilli and pepper deboned leg of lamb on the braai

Pepper, chilli and lamb go so well together. This is a quick and easy, yet very impressive-looking dish to prepare on the braai*. You need a good bed of coals and a moderate to high heat (if you can hold your hand 10 cm above the grid and count to five, the coals are ready; if you don't get to five, they are still too hot).

1 deboned leg of lamb, butterflied
Lots of cracked black pepper –
    enough to cover whole roast
1 handful chopped fresh chili
1 handful coarse sea salt
Olive oil

Make sure the leg is cut so that it resembles a large, flattish chopping board. Make a rub by combining all the ingredients and cover the meat, working the rub into all the cracks and crevices. Place in a marinating dish and refrigerate overnight.

Two hours before you are ready to braai, remove the meat from the fridge and allow to come back to room temperature. When the coals are at the correct temperature, place the meat on the grill for about 30 minutes, turning frequently until the meat is nice and pink inside.

Once done, allow to rest for 10 minutes. Place on a chopping board and slice thinly with a sharp knife. Serve with prune and chilli salad (see page 125) and a chilled Bukettraube.

SERVES 6–8

* If you really feel the need to cook this in the oven, roast at 180 °C for about 20 minutes per 500 g for medium (which you want it to be).

Deboned shoulder of lamb and venison roasted with peaches, rosemary and thyme

This is a really tasty variation of a classic shoulder roast. Ask your butcher to debone the shoulders if you are not confident enough to do it yourself.

I like to put the venison roast at the bottom with the fatty lamb on top so that the lamb juices can drip into the venison. I tie the roasts together with string or use butcher's netting with a layer of fresh herbs and peaches sandwiched in between to ensure a lovely flavour infusion and that all-important sweetness that venison loves so much. Try to keep this dish as simple as possible as the natural meat flavours are fantastic and you don't want to spoil them by adding too many flavours.

1 lamb shoulder roast, deboned and butterflied
1 venison shoulder roast, deboned and butterflied
Olive oil
Salt and freshly ground pepper
1 large handful fresh thyme
1 large handful fresh rosemary
2 peaches, depipped and chopped (you can cheat and use canned peaches if you want)
6–8 potatoes, peeled and quartered

Preheat the oven to 180 °C.

Score the fatty side of the lamb roast with a sharp knife to help release the fat during the cooking process. Rub both roasts with olive oil and season with salt and pepper. Cover one side of the venison with the thyme, rosemary and peaches, and then place the lamb roast on top, fatty side up. Tie the roasts together with string or stuff into butcher's netting.

Place into a roasting pan, surround with potatoes and roast, uncovered, for 1½–2 hours, basting occasionally with the pan juices, until the meat is tender and can be pulled off the roast easily with your fingers.

Once cooked, remove from the roasting pan and allow to rest for 20 minutes. Slice, ensuring you mix the two meats together.

Beautiful, beautiful, beautiful!

SERVES 6–8

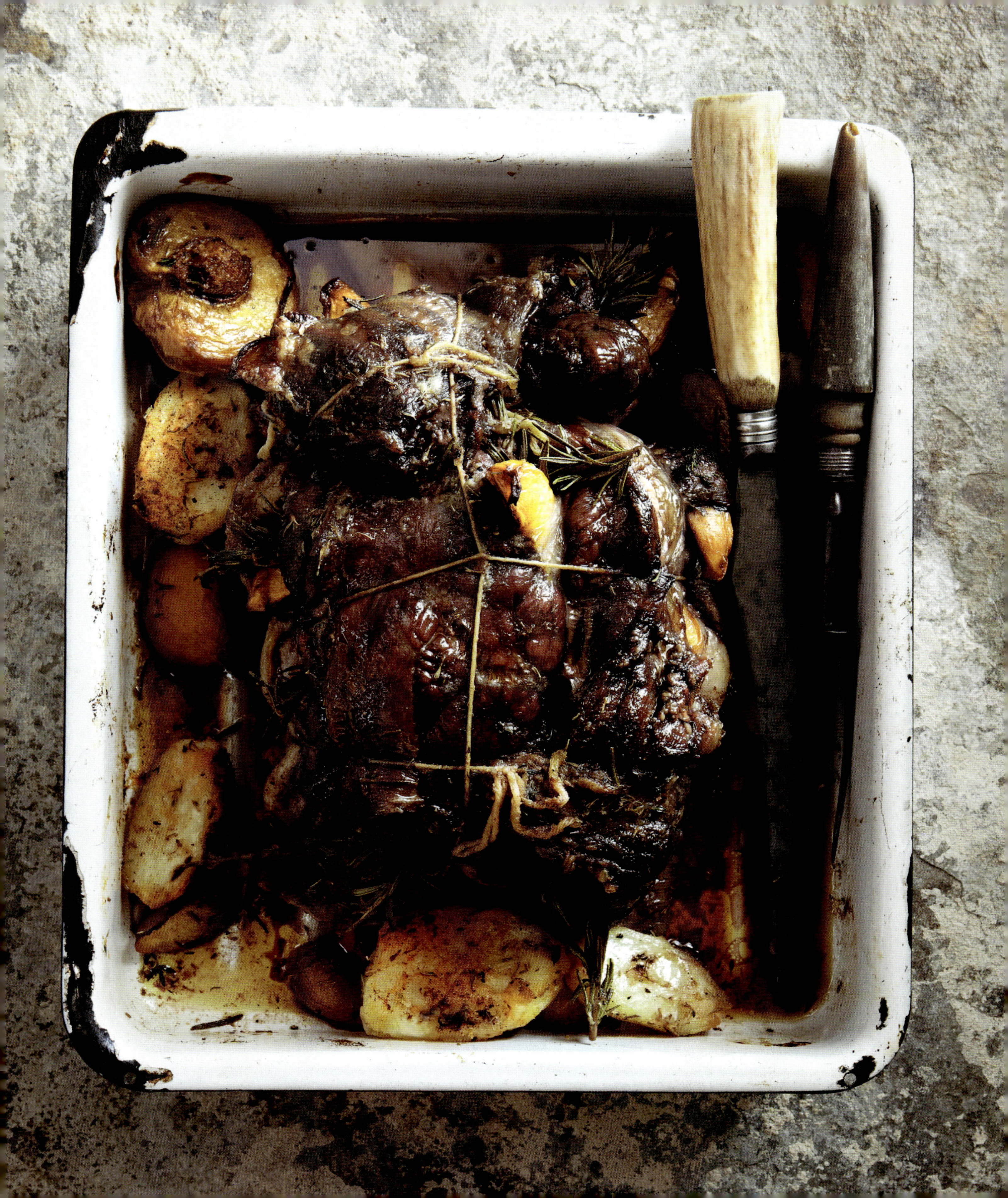

Nguni Beef

Shortly after moving to Graaff-Reinet, we met some of the Nguni breeders in the area. Until then I thought that all beef was pretty much the same. Silly me. As I discovered, there is a massive difference in the texture and flavour of the meat of the various breeds.

Our new friends Kevin Watermeyer, a deep-thinking conservation farmer, and his wife Lisa and their two children, have established one of the better Nguni studs in southern Africa on his Zuurplaats farmstead deep in the Sneeuberg mountains on the way to Nieu-Bethesda.

Trenly and Wilmari Spence are also Nguni breeders. Trenly is the determination behind their family farm Kriegerskraal (which has been in the Spence family for over a century) outside Graaff-Reinet and was the first person to introduce Ngunis to the area. Despite years of drought, tough farming conditions and severe criticism from his commercial farming peers, his holistic farming practices and dogged determination have resulted in a win-win situation for both his cattle and the land they utilise.

Kevin and Trenly's farms are a showcase of how humans and nature can co-exist in a mutually symbiotic relationship. They use no supplementation, no chemical treatments, no dipping or dosing, no hormonal treatments and no growth stimulants. This flies in the face of the theories of many large commercial farmers and is not without its critics.

They and many like-minded farmers in the area certainly have my admiration and support. Ever since meeting these guys, I have been sold on this diminutive and incredibly beautiful African breed of cattle.

South Africa's indigenous Nguni cattle, long the mainstay of traditional Zulu culture, are possibly the most beautiful cattle in the world. They are perfectly adapted to the vegetation and climate of the continent and thus thrive in the harsh Karoo veld with ease.

All the associated flavour benefits discussed in the lamb chapter on pages 28–29 apply here too, and there is very little that needs to be added to this beef to bring out its best. The meat of African breeds also tends to be a lot leaner than that of the Red European breeds that seem to dominate South Africa's beef industry.

Any cooks worth their salt know that when it comes to preparing the perfect steak, timing is everything. If undercooked it will be cold, chewy and miserable, and if overdone it will be tough and dry. Though there are some who may disagree, in my opinion overcooked steak is unkind to and dishonours the animal. Personally, I love my beef from rare to medium at most, hot or cold, depending on what I am serving it with and, of course, depending on the time of year.

That said, however, a slow-cooked, old-fashioned red curry in mid-winter, served with chopped fresh coriander, also has its merits.

Regardless of how you like your beef, please always remember that an animal gave its life so that you can have food on your table, so treat it with the respect and dignity it deserves. And what better way to do that than to go out and find a veld-raised, organic piece of beef to cook up and give a royal send-off, toasted, of course, with a lovely glass of good Cape wine. That's the stuff!

NGUNI BEEF 47

Flash-fried *pap en sous* balls with Nguni mince

I have no real basis for this recipe except to say that it is a fairly eccentric take on the classic pap en sous *(mealie meal porridge and relish) that is such a staple of the Karoo and South African diet. I am mad about* pap en sous *but felt it needed a bit of an upgrade. My version is great as a small starter or finger food snack. I find that everyone thinks I'm completely mad when I first explain it to them, until they taste it. And then they absolutely love it.*

Please play around with the ingredients and substitute whatever you fancy, or leave out the meat if you want to do a vegetarian version. Remember, this is a fun dish so have fun with it! I like to use Nguni mince as it is not fatty, but venison works beautifully too. The main point is to make sure you use lean mince.

PAP BALLS
500 g cooked (as per instructions on packet) stiff mealie meal (*stywe pap*)
30 ml mild curry powder
150 g cooked Nguni beef mince
65 g Parmesan cheese, grated
2 teaspoons dried mixed herbs
30 g feta cheese, crumbled
1 egg, beaten
Fresh breadcrumbs
Cooking oil for deep-frying

RELISH
1 onion, finely chopped
2 cloves garlic, chopped
Olive oil
2 tomatoes, peeled and chopped
1 handful chopped fresh basil

To make the *pap* balls, mix the warm *pap* with the remaining ingredients, except the egg and breadcrumbs. Roll the mixture into equal-sized balls. Dip in the egg, then roll in the crumbs. Refrigerate for 30 minutes to set.

Make the relish whilst your balls are settling (that sounds terrible, but you know what I mean). Gently sweat the onion and garlic in a glug of olive oil, then add the tomatoes and simmer for 10 minutes until everything is soft. Remove from the heat and immediately stir in the basil.

Fill a small saucepan about halfway with cooking oil and heat to about 190 °C (if you drop a few breadcrumbs into the oil they should fizzle immediately and rise to the top). Once the oil is ready, pop the balls in, a few at a time, for 10–15 seconds or until golden. Remove and place on paper towel to drain.

Place a nice spoonful of the tomato and onion relish on each serving plate. Top with one or two balls and serve immediately. They taste even better when you eat them with your fingers.

YOU CAN MAKE 10–15 BALLS PER 500 G OF *PAP* (adjust quantities accordingly)

NGUNI BEEF 49

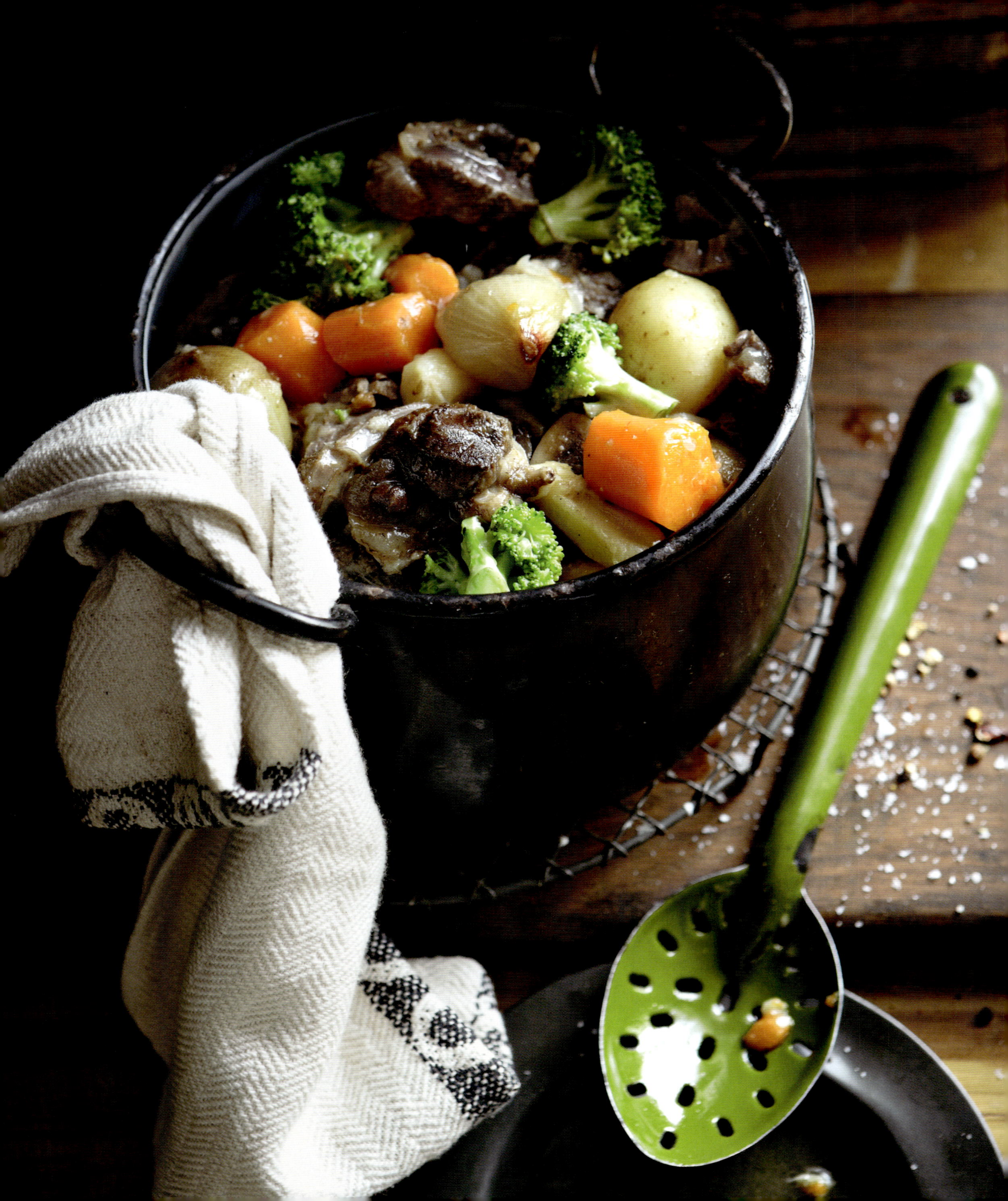

Beef casserole with parsnips and baby jacket potatoes

Anyone who likes beef loves a good stew. When I am feeling like I am coming down with the flu or early in winter when the family starts to hint at getting the sniffles, I like to make this casserole. I prefer to use shin as it is full of flavour and stickiness and the natural collagen in the connective tissue is not only a superb immune booster but also helps to thicken up the sauce as well as help your body assimilate and utilise all the vitamin C from the carrots. The parsnips (one of my favourite veg) give it a sort of nutty flavour and, together with the jacket potatoes, are full of potassium. The pickling onions sweeten up nicely and are packed full of antioxidants, and everyone knows that garlic and broccoli are super foods. Who says healthy food can't be tasty and comforting?

Olive oil
6 pickling onions, peeled
6 cloves garlic, peeled
1 kg beef shin
Salt and freshly ground pepper
2 carrots, peeled and roughly chopped
2 parsnips, peeled and roughly chopped
8 baby jacket potatoes, washed
1 handful chopped fresh herbs (rosemary, marjoram, thyme, oregano), plus extra for garnishing
500 ml good-quality beef stock
5 broccoli florets

Preheat the oven to 180 °C.

Heat a dash of oil in a stovetop-to-oven casserole and brown the onions and garlic. Add the meat and brown this too, seasoning as you go. Once browned, add the remaining ingredients (except the broccoli), give it all a good stir, pop the lid on and place in the oven for 1½ hours.

Add the broccoli, give it a gentle stir and return to the oven for 30 minutes.

Serve with a sprinkling of the fresh herbs over the top.

SERVES 4–6

Beef stir-fry with baby cabbage and seeds galore

This is a very quick and easy dish that can be whipped up in minutes and will be a whole lot tastier and healthier for you than a take-away. We often eat it as is, as a late night, post-party snack. And believe me, the antioxidants in all those nuts will help you the next morning.

The pan-seared beef strips will benefit from a dash of soy sauce; don't add salt though, as it won't be necessary.

500 g beef strips
Soy sauce
Peanut oil
1 handful mixed seeds and nuts
½ green baby cabbage, chopped
½ red baby cabbage, chopped
2 cloves garlic, chopped
1 chilli, deseeded and chopped
Freshly ground pepper

Place the beef strips in a marinating dish and sprinkle with soy sauce. Allow to marinate while you chop the veg.

In a hot pan or wok, add some oil and quickly brown the seeds and nuts. Remove from the pan and set aside. Toss in the beef and brown for 2 minutes, stirring constantly. Add the cabbage, garlic and chilli, and toss about for another 3 minutes. The cabbage should be crisp, not soggy. Add pepper to taste.

Remove from the heat and toss in the seeds. Serve immediately.

Now off to bed with a large glass of water.

SERVES 2

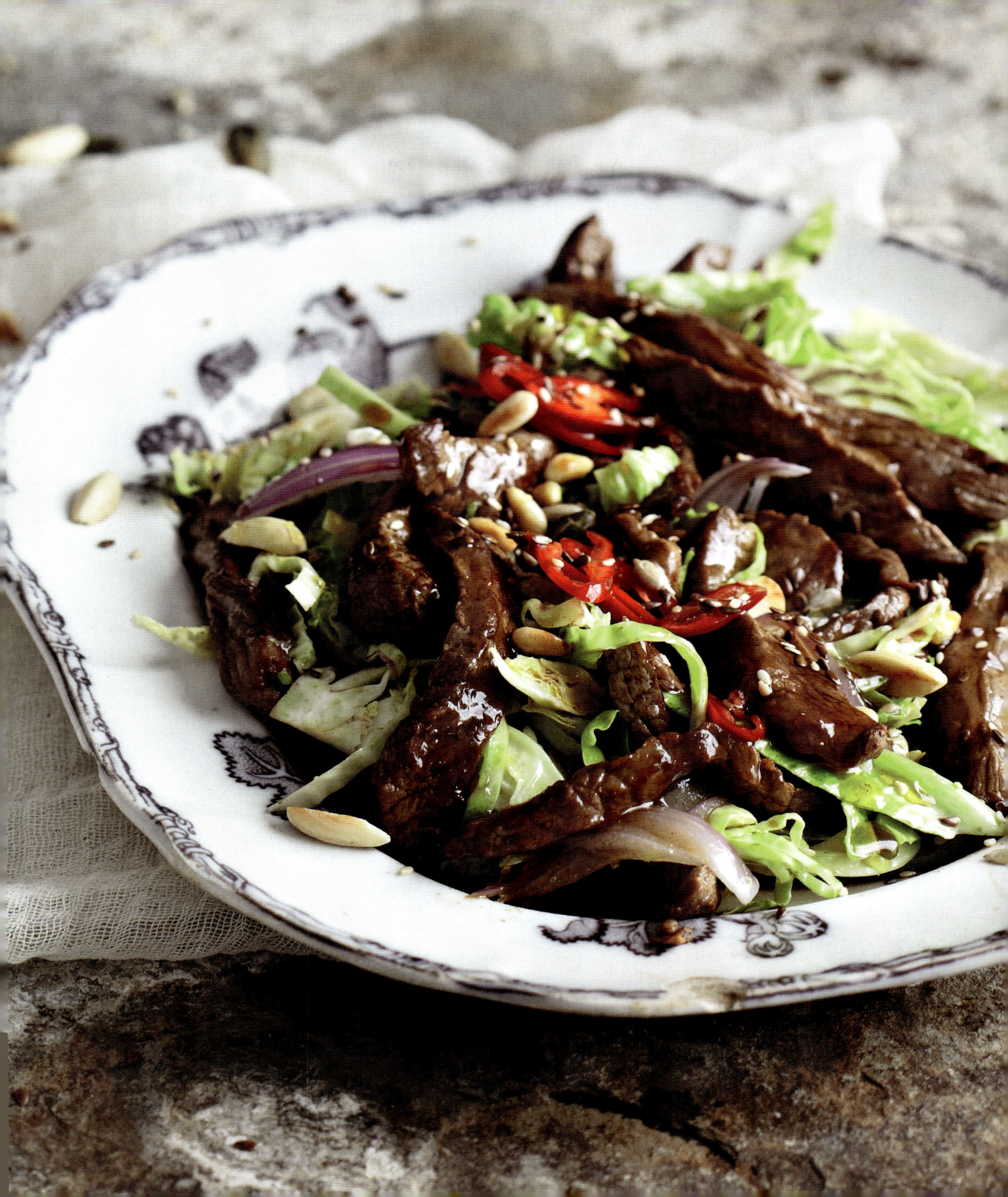

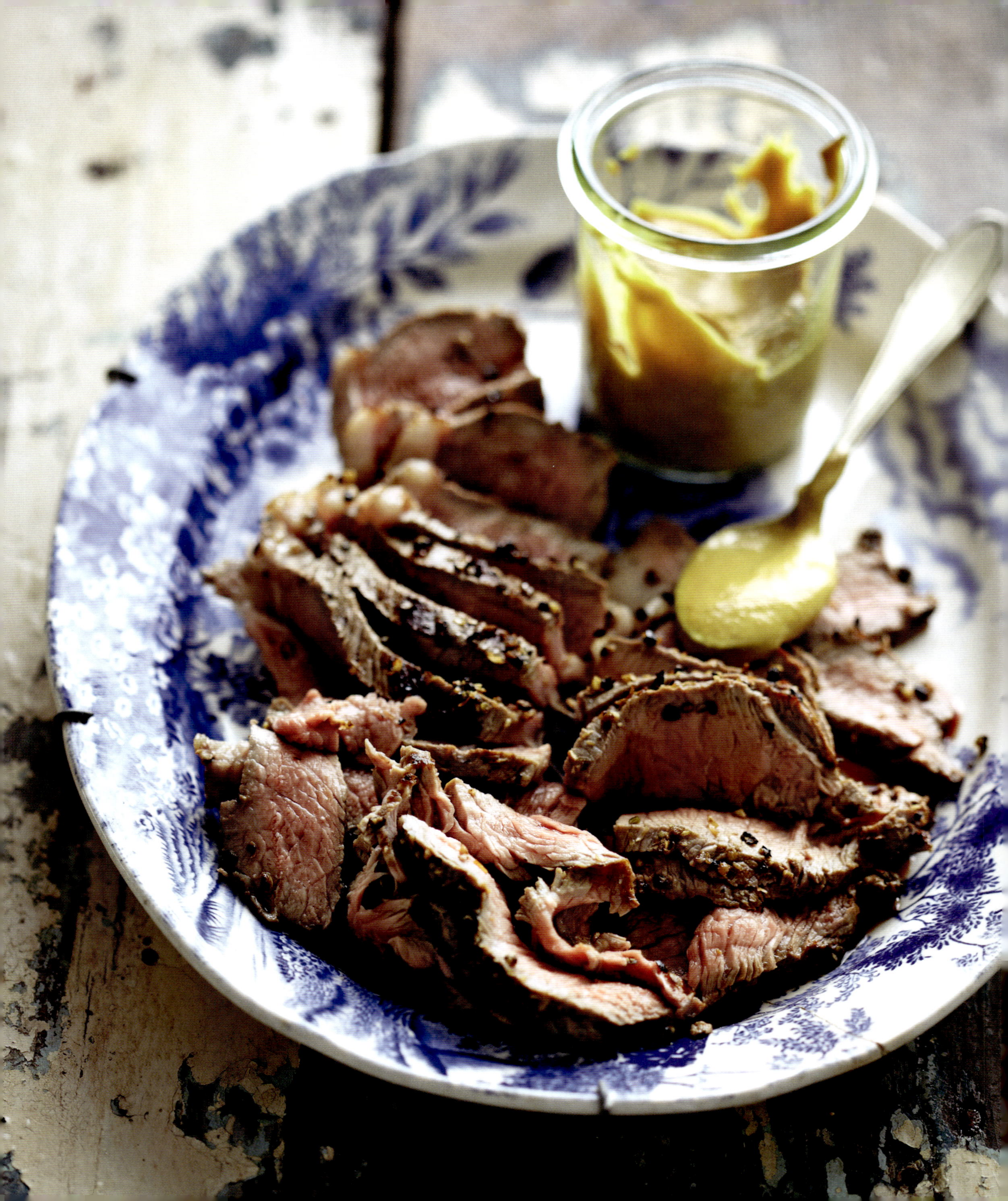

Spicy crusted whole barbecued rump

I did this for my whiskey club (see pic on page 7) one evening and it was a roaring success. It will easily feed 10 hungry people so adjust the size of the rump according to how many people you want to feed – a rough guide is to have 300 g of meat per man and 150 g per woman. I like to cook this in my kettle braai over an indirect heat (25 briquettes on each side). You can also do it in the oven, at 180 °C, but it won't have that same smoky taste. As usual, cook for 20 minutes per 500 g for medium.

This recipe also works great with venison, so if you have a nice kudu rump use that instead, just be sure not to overcook it. Medium-rare is best.

1 whole matured rump (± 3.5 kg)
Olive oil

RUB
50 g cracked black pepper
30 g cracked coriander seeds
50 g coarse salt
30 ml mustard powder
50 g finely chopped fresh rosemary
4 fresh chillies, chopped

It is very important that the meat is well matured and at room temperature, so be sure to take it out of the fridge early enough.

Mix all the rub ingredients together. Rub a generous quantity of olive oil all over the meat, followed by the spicy rub to form a thin crust. Sear the meat in a super-hot griddle pan or similar until well browned. Transfer immediately to the kettle braai, close the lid and cook for 20 minutes per 500 g (or an internal temperature of 63 °C) for medium-rare.

Once ready, remove from the heat and rest for 10 minutes before slicing. Scrumptious with a good peaty single malt!

Arno's rare spiced rump with mustard

My great mates Arno and Tracy Bouwer love to braai in summer around their pool. Arno loves his steak really rare and rump steak is so full of flavour and texture that we love to do it this way on a hot summer's day, grilled on the braai or even in a pan. The coriander and pepper crust gives it a bit of extra spice. Serve cold and thinly sliced and with a dash of strong mustard. It's great for a casual outdoorsy lunch with a leafy summer salad.

1 thick-cut rump steak (750 g–1 kg)
Olive oil
1 handful cracked black pepper
1 handful cracked coriander seeds
1 pot strong English mustard

Rub the steak generously with oil and then the pepper and coriander seeds. Allow to stand for about 1 hour to reach room temperature.

Grill over really hot coals (or in a pan) for 4 minutes per side until the meat is sealed. Remove from the heat immediately and set aside to rest and cool completely.

Once cooled, slice very thinly (across the grain) with a sharp knife. Serve on a large chopping board with the meat juices poured over, a good dollop of the mustard on the side and the marinated prune and chilli salad (see page 125). Oh, and don't forget the wine …

1 LARGE RUMP WILL BE ENOUGH FOR 4–6 PEOPLE (if you slice it thinly)

Spade flambéed sirloin with mushrooms and asparagus

This is a really fun and cool way to prepare sirloin. My mate Graham Harris and I did this one Mother's Day to surprise the ladies. They thought we were completely mad, but absolutely loved the show and the end result.

It is really impressive around the camp or braai fire with a group of mates, but you do need an able braai assistant to help you, as one person needs to manage the spade while the other manages the meat and pours the beer.

The first time we did it we actually used a whole kudu sirloin, but have since done it again and again using everything from springbok to beef. As this is the beef section, you get the beef version.

---

1 whole beef sirloin
Thick soy sauce (or Worcestershire sauce if you prefer)
Black pepper
4 cloves garlic, finely chopped
Olive oil
1 punnet portabellini mushrooms, halved
1 bunch asparagus spears, washed and halved
125 ml brandy
Knob of butter mixed with flour (*beurre manié*)

Find a clean spade (I prefer the deep builder's-type spade) and wash and scrub it thoroughly.

Baste the sirloin with soy sauce and then rub on the black pepper and garlic. Coat with a little olive oil.

Heat up the spade over a nice hot fire (you need a little bit of flame), being sure to keep the handle away from the heat so you don't burn your hands whilst holding it. When the spade is really hot, get your mate to put the sirloin in the scoop of the spade and seal the meat all over. Don't put any oil in the spade as the oil on the meat is enough to do the job.

Once the meat is sealed, move the spade a little higher so that the meat can cook without burning. Cook for 5 minutes per side (4 sides + 20 minutes). Arrange the mushrooms and asparagus around the meat and let them cook in the meat juices for a further 5 minutes. Pour over the brandy and quickly ignite it. (Look out for your eyebrows!)

Once the flames go out, remove from the heat and place the meat one side to rest, together with the asparagus and mushrooms. Thicken up the pan juices with a knob of butter mixed with some flour (add slowly and stir until the correct consistency is reached).

Place the sirloin on a large cutting board, cover with mushrooms and asparagus, and pour over the sauce. Get your braai buddy and take a bow – ta-dah!

2.5 KG SIRLOIN SHOULD FEED 8–10 PEOPLE

The first real friends we made when we visited the Karoo were the Harrises.

We met the Harris family when I dragged my own family along on a hunting trip to the Karoo in 2007. We were living in Port Elizabeth and I was on the local committee of the South African Hunters and Game Conservation Association (www.sahunters.co.za) at the time. The Aberdeen hunting club (Aberdeen is a small town about 60 km south of Graaff-Reinet) was doing a fundraiser, which I helped to promote for them, and as a thank you they offered me a weekend hunt with a few local farmers in the Kendrew district near Graaff-Reinet for a very good price.

When I called up a certain Mr Graham Harris one evening to arrange the trip, he had no idea who I was or what I was talking about. Only after much explaining and memory jogging did he vaguely remember something about offering a hunt to the Aberdeen hunting club months before. Despite it all being very hazy and the explanation coming from a dubious fellow from PE, in true Harris style he told me that he would arrange something and I should come on the last weekend of August. 'Oh, and bring the family. I also have kids, so maybe they will get on.'

By the end of an absolutely wonderful hunting and family weekend on their farm Taainjiesview, the kids were exhausted but happy, and Rose and Helen, Graham and I were friends for life. Unbeknownst to all of us at the time, we were to move to the Karoo less than six months later.

Easy-peasy shoulder roast

This is such an easy Sunday roast. All you really need is a decent shoulder roast (I like the end cut of a shoulder of beef), some wine, a few herbs and a leisurely Sunday.

- 250 ml white wine
- 2 sprigs fresh rosemary
- 1 beef shoulder (2.5 kg)
- Salt and freshly ground pepper
- 3 sprigs fresh thyme
- 1 Sunday paper (preferably one with no bad news …)

Preheat the oven to 240 °C.

Pour the wine into a suitable casserole dish, add some rosemary and then the roast. Sprinkle with salt and pepper and add the thyme. Put the lid on the casserole dish and place in the very hot oven for 10 minutes. Reduce the oven temperature to 160 °C.

Take the Sunday paper and read it on the stoep (veranda) for about 1½ hours, or until the meat is soft and tender and falling off the bone.

Remove from the oven and allow to rest for 10 minutes while you use the pan juices to make a gravy (see below). Serve with roasted potatoes, crisp garden vegetables and a good red wine.

Finish off with an afternoon snooze. Now that's a Sunday well spent.

SERVES 4–6

How to make gravy

Once you have removed your roast from the roasting pan and set it aside to rest, scrape all the sticky bits from the bottom of the pan and return the pan to the stovetop over medium heat. Add a little water (dependent on how much gravy you want) and stir everything up nicely. That's where all the goodness and flavour is. Remove the hard, woody bits and mash up any softer bits. If you can find a bit of cooked potato mash that up and use it to thicken the gravy. Alternatively, place 10 ml cornflour into 125 ml cold milk (or water) and stir it up before adding slowly to the gravy to thicken. Allow to simmer for a few minutes and season to taste as you go.

NGUNI BEEF 59

Oxtail curry

A version of the winter classic that Rose and I came up with one winter. It was a cold and miserable day and we were really in the mood for comfort food but did not fancy going outside or to the shops so had to make do with what we had in the cupboard. We had been on a bit of a spicy food binge at the time, hence the Eastern theme with the spices. It turned out famously and has been our favourite oxtail recipe ever since.

That first time we only had eland tail and used that, but of course not everyone has access to eland. Oxtail has more meat and works wonderfully, but if you have eland, definitely use that. If you have both, then you are truly blessed.

This recipe makes enough to feed a family of four quite comfortably. Any leftovers can be frozen for the next rainy day.

Olive oil
1 whole bulb garlic, chopped
1 thumb-length piece of fresh ginger, finely chopped
2 kg oxtail
20 ml chilli powder
3 cardamom pods
5 ml ground coriander
5 ml ground cumin
5 ml ground cinnamon
1 can (410 g) baked beans
1 can (410 g) coconut milk
Salt and freshly ground pepper
500 ml water
1 handful fresh coriander

Heat a little olive oil in a heavy-based, flat-bottomed pot and sweat off the garlic and ginger. Brown the oxtail pieces and then remove from the pot and set aside. Add the rest of the ingredients, except the water and coriander, and heat gently whilst stirring.

Once hot, return the oxtail to the pot, add the water, put the lid on and simmer for 2–3 hours, stirring occasionally, until the meat is soft. Once done, remove from the heat and leave it to cool completely. (Ideally you want to leave it overnight, as this really allows the flavours to develop and everyone knows that the best curries are made the day before.)

Reheat over low heat for 1 hour before serving with chopped fresh coriander and steamed basmati or jasmine rice.

SERVES 4–6

Two-buck chuck pot roast

Beef chuck or braising steak is one of the cheaper or sub-prime cuts, yet has such a good balance of meat and fat that if cooked correctly it can be one of the tastiest and tenderest roasts you will ever have. You will usually find it at your butcher as a thickish bone-in chuck steak, and it is really good for stewing. It comes from the top part of the shoulder, behind the neck, and if you ask your butcher to cut you a chuck roast, you will probably get a decent size roast (enough to feed 4–5 people) with some shoulder bone and a bit of top rib as well.

In the USA they call this a seven-bone roast. This is not a bad thing though as all those bones add so much flavour. The old saying about the meat closest to the bone being the sweetest is completely true. I like to call this my two-buck chuck roast because it's really month-end affordable, but such a treat. Just cook it nice and slow and you're good to go!

1 chuck roast (1.5–2 kg)
Black pepper
Dried mixed herbs
Cracked coriander seeds
Mustard powder
Olive oil
Thick soy sauce
500 ml beef stock
3 cloves garlic
2 sprigs fresh rosemary
6 whole roasting potatoes

Use a flat-bottomed cast-iron pot or heavy stovetop-to-oven casserole dish and place it in the oven at 240 °C to heat up while you prepare the meat.

Using a mortar and pestle, add the black pepper, mixed herbs, coriander seeds and mustard powder, and grind until fine. Add some olive oil to form a thin paste.

Rub some soy sauce over the meat (if you salt the meat before sealing it it can make it tough, so I like to use soy sauce as this gives the cut saltiness and colour without toughening it up). Rub the herby paste all over the roast, being sure to get it into all the crevices.

Remove the pot from the oven – be careful, it's hot! Add the roast and seal all over very quickly. Add the stock, garlic and rosemary and return to the oven for 10 minutes.

After 10 minutes, toss in the potatoes, reduce the oven temperature to 160 °C and roast for 2 hours with the lid on. Once cooked and soft, remove the roast and set aside to rest.

Remove the potatoes, cut them in half and place back in the oven, cut side down, with a good drizzle of olive oil, at 260 °C* to get all golden and crispy.

Whilst the taters are crisping, use the same pot with the meat juices and stock to make a gravy (see page 58).

Serve with the roast potatoes, steamed carrots and some crisp broccoli.

* If your oven doesn't have a temperature setting this high, simply set it to the highest oven temperature you have and roast until the potatoes are golden and crisp.

SERVES 4–6

Rolled beef fillet stuffed with pine nuts, spinach and mushrooms

When you need to impress someone – maybe the boss is coming over for dinner – here is a pretty easy but pretty impressive-looking and tasty way of doing a beef fillet.

Fillet is generally the tenderest cut; the down side is that it does not have too much flavour, so any help you can give it will always be welcome. The mushrooms and spinach add depth of flavour and the pine nuts add an interesting texture. All are, of course, super healthy.

---

1 whole fillet (1–1.5 kg)
75 g pine nuts
Knob of butter
200 g mushrooms, finely chopped
　(I prefer the meaty brown or wild mushrooms)
250 g chopped spinach
4 cloves garlic, finely chopped
A few sprigs fresh thyme and rosemary
100 g feta cheese, crumbled (optional)

Place the fillet on a large chopping board and, using a meat mallet, flatten the fillet until it is about 3 cm thick.

In a dry pan, lightly roast the pine nuts. Remove from the pan and set aside.

Heat the butter in the same pan and lightly fry the mushrooms, spinach and garlic with the herbs for about 5 minutes – the spinach should just start to wilt. Once the mix is heated through, set aside to cool.

Once cooled, layer the mushroom and spinach mix onto the flattened fillet and top with the feta, if using, and pine nuts. Roll up tightly into a long loaf shape. Tie the fillet with string at regular intervals to keep it from coming apart. (You may need an extra pair of hands for this.) Finally, wrap the whole rolled fillet tightly in plastic wrap and refrigerate for at least 1 hour to allow it to keep its shape. It should look like a big meaty Swiss roll by now.

Preheat the oven to 180 °C.

When ready to cook, remove the fillet from the plastic wrap and seal carefully in a very hot pan. Place the fillet in an uncovered roasting dish in the oven for 20 minutes (medium-rare) or longer if you want it done more. (You don't!)

Once done, remove from the oven and allow to rest, wrapped in foil, for 5 minutes. Slice crossways so that you have medallions of beautifully pink beef with the filling just oozing out.

Serve on top of mini potato bakes (see page 126) with crisp steamed baby carrots on the side, and a bold Pinotage.

Should be good for a decent salary increase come review time …

IF YOU USE A WHOLE FILLET, YOU WILL FEED 6–8 PEOPLE

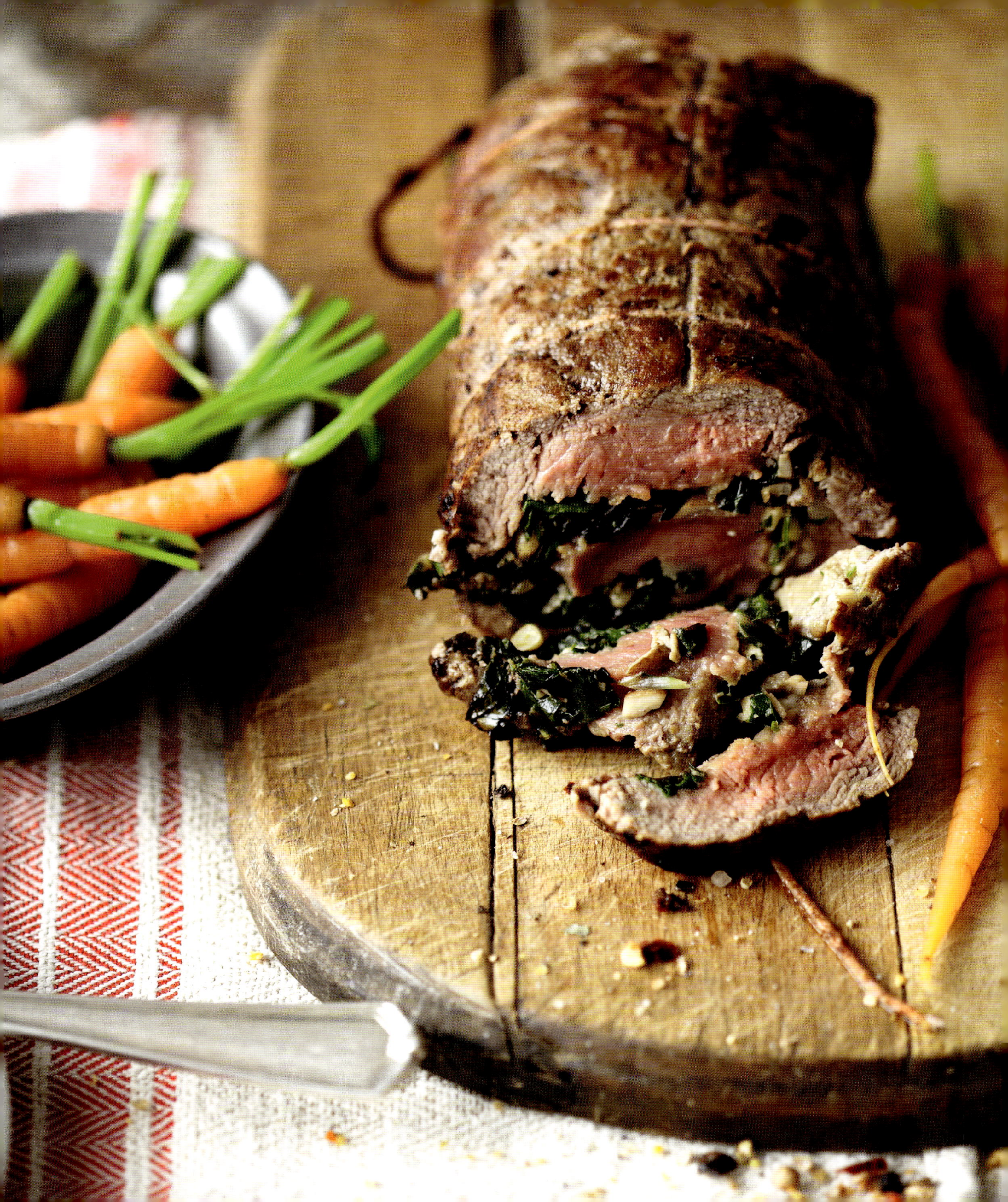

Free-range Chicken

We know a lovely lady by the name of Linda Charles, who farms with her husband Garth on the Kendrew Estates about 35 km from Graaff-Reinet. Linda rears the most delicious, plump and tasty chickens I have ever eaten, with the result that I only use her wonderful produce in my restaurant, delivered fresh by Linda herself. With such lovely chicken, so full of flavour, I had no choice but to develop some recipes to do it justice. Whenever Linda comes into town with my delivery, delicious recipe ideas race through my head. It is, however, the fresh herbs in my garden that influence what I will be making with each batch. There is so much to be said for good old-fashioned roast chicken, the way Granny used to do it. Post war, there was very little meat available so chicken was a special Sunday treat, and rightly so. The skin all crisp and golden and the flesh tender and succulent and irresistible, especially when accompanied by crispy roasted potatoes.

Whenever you buy chicken, try to buy the best quality that you can afford. Local markets are springing up all over the place and are a wonderful setting in which to find fresh organic chickens at good prices. By supporting these local producers you also help stimulate your local economy and ensure a good and steady supply of reasonably priced quality produce.

The other upside to this is that you generally get to meet the farmers/producers in person, so can find out exactly how humanely the chickens were raised and what they were fed. It's a win for both you and the farmer.

FREE-RANGE CHICKEN

Slow-roasted basil chicken

I got a similar idea from one of my food heroes, Jamie Oliver, where he stuffs chopped herbs under the skin of the breasts. He has such an obvious passion for what he does and he really wears his heart on his sleeve. We are of similar age and I enjoy the way he throws himself into cooking and makes it such fun – which it is. I believe cooking should be good, honest fun and as simple as possible.

Roast chicken is one of the all-time classics. All through the ages, from the time of the caveman, when he roasted his first bird on the very first fire, through the rise and fall of the Roman Empire, the Dark Ages, the Renaissance and to the modern era, humankind has always searched for the perfect roast chicken. Okay, I may be exaggerating a tad, but you get the gist.

We love roast chicken and now I have one of the best recipes in the history of roast chicken-kind for you. It works really well in the oven, but is absolutely superb cooked in the kettle braai over indirect heat with 25 briquettes on either side. Try it, you'll be convinced. Thanks for the inspiration Jamie.

---

1 whole chicken
10 fresh basil leaves
6 fresh sage leaves
A good dollop of olive oil
5 sprigs fresh rosemary (finely chop 1 sprig)
Coarse salt
Cracked black pepper
½ lemon

Using your finger, carefully separate the skin from the breasts and slide the basil and sage leaves in-between.

Make sure the skin is nice and dry, then pour a dollop of oil into a mortar and pestle, add the chopped rosemary, salt and pepper and a squeeze of lemon, and give it a good stir. Using your hands, rub this mixture all over the bird, then salt and pepper the cavity and stuff the lemon and rosemary sprigs inside. Truss up with string so that everything does not fall out.

When the kettle braai or oven is hot (the oven should be preheated to 230 °C), pop the bird on a roasting tray and roast for about 1½ hours, or until it is crisp and golden and the legs pull free easily. Take out and leave to rest for 15 minutes before carving.

Serve with roasted potatoes, roasted veg and gravy made from the pan juices (see page 58).

SERVES 4

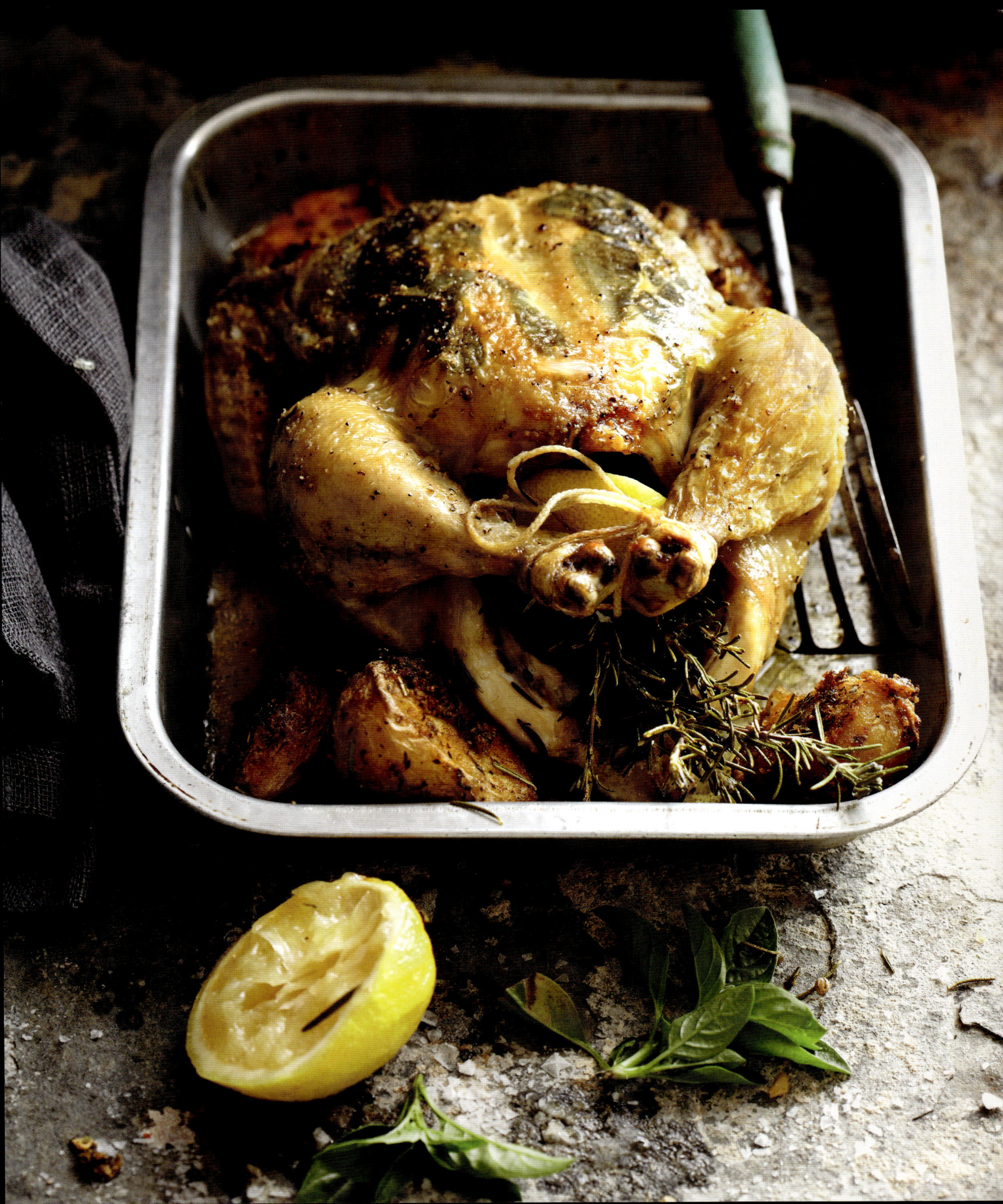

Chicken in goop

I used to eat a very similar dish when I was still at school and dating the first love of my life, an intelligent and cute blonde named Wendy Green. Her mom used to make it often and I would try to get myself invited for lunch whenever she made it. I never really knew how she made it or what went into it but it has remained one of my favourite comfort dishes of all time.

I had tried to replicate it over the years, but never got it right. After we married, Rose used to get very frustrated with me because all I could explain (in an exasperated tone) was that it was 'chicken in a goopy sauce'. One year Rose and I visited close friends Cara and John McEwan's folks in Plettenberg Bay and Cara's mom, Colleen Kemp, presented us with this dish for lunch.

I immediately exclaimed to Rose: 'Look, it's chicken in goop!' The whole table thought I was having an alcohol-induced fit but Rose knew exactly what I was talking about and we made Colleen tell us how she made it. Imagine my surprise when I learned how simple it was. This is my version.

6–8 chicken pieces (I prefer to use drums and thighs)
250 ml fruit chutney
250 ml good-quality mayonnaise
400 g jar quinces (or 1 can of apricots – you can decide)
5–10 ml curry powder

Preheat the oven to 180 °C.

Place the chicken pieces in an ovenproof baking dish.

Mix the chutney, mayonnaise, juice from the bottled/canned fruit and the curry powder together. Pour over the chicken pieces and bake for about 1 hour. Add the fruit and bake for another 15 minutes.

My family is currently into brown rice, so we have it with that, otherwise you could serve it on fluffy mashed potatoes or any other starch of choice. You will definitely need something to soak up the goop …

SERVES 4

One-pot chicken and veg casserole

This is a wonderfully flavourful one-pot meal that is a real bash-and-dash special (you bash it all into the pot and dash off to do whatever you need to do). It works famously in a slow-cooker or crock pot. You can bash it into the slow-cooker before work, dash off and come home to a lovely steaming dinner. I prefer to do it in a casserole dish in the oven, but you decide.

I also put whatever vegetables are in season into the pot so don't worry too much if you can't find some of the veg listed here; just substitute with what you have and if you are afraid of garlic tone it down to how you like it.

I roughly chop all the vegetables so it makes for a nice chunky dish and use as much or as little as I like, depending how many I am feeding at the time. The only thing you need to be careful with is when you add the cream. Pour it in slowly, a little at a time, stirring continuously to ensure it does not curdle due to the acidity of the tomatoes. Otherwise it's plain sailing and very, very tasty.

Dash of olive oil
Knob of butter
1 whole bulb garlic, **finely chopped**
10 pickling onions, peeled
1 whole chicken, portioned
1 handful fresh sage
1 handful fresh rosemary
5 ripe tomatoes, chopped
500 ml chicken stock
200 g pearled wheat
150 ml fresh cream (optional)
1 can (410 g) peach slices
Red pepper
Courgettes
Aubergines
Carrots
Green beans
Parsnips
Pinch of coarse salt

Preheat the oven to 160 °C (unless you're using a slow-cooker).

Heat the olive oil and butter in a stovetop-to-oven casserole dish and brown the garlic and onions.

Add the chicken, sage and rosemary, and brown. Add the tomatoes, chicken stock and pearled wheat. Gradually add the cream, if using, stirring continuously to prevent curdling. Add the remaining ingredients.

Transfer to the oven and bake with the lid on for 1½ hours, or until well cooked. If you're using a slow-cooker, set to auto shift and leave it to gently simmer away for day.

What could be easier?

MAKES ENOUGH TO FEED 6–8 PEOPLE (leftovers can be kept for sandwiches the next day)

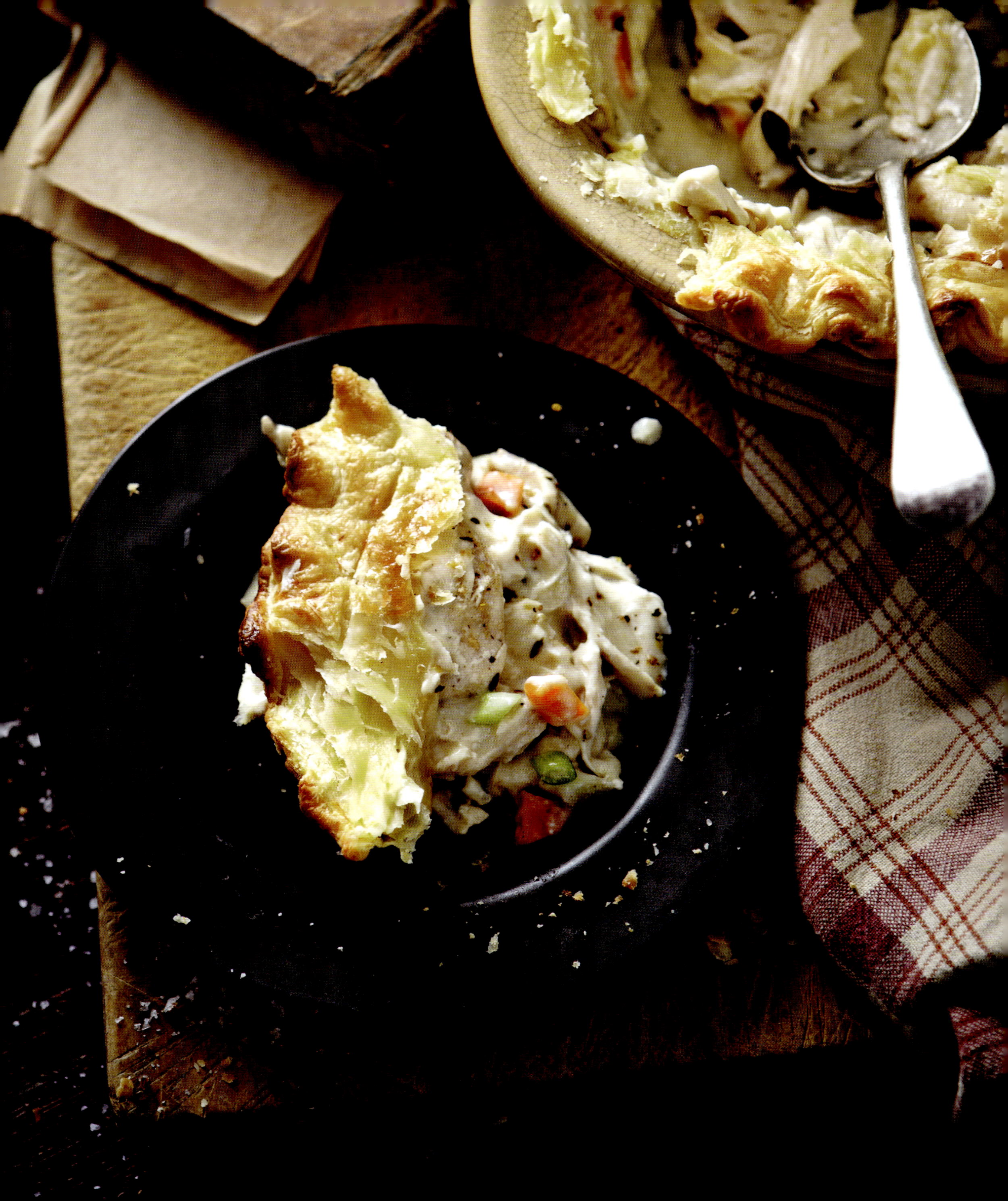

Herby chicken pie

Chicken takes to fresh herbs like the proverbial duck to water. It carries the flavours so well and I love infusing my chicken pies with fragrant chicken-friendly herbs such as basil, marjoram and sage. This gives you a saucy, fragrant piece of pie instead of the sticky flavourless glop that often seems to pass for a chicken pie nowadays.

This recipe is great for making a large family-sized pie or a few small individual pies that can be stored in the freezer for when you fancy a quick yet tasty meal. Just whip out a frozen pie, pop straight into the oven at 180 °C until golden brown and you have a deliciously herby and crisp meal ready to eat.

The milk in this recipe helps to gently infuse and tenderise the chicken and adds to the wonderful sauce at the end.

---

1 good-sized knob butter
1 handful fresh sage leaves
1 handful fresh basil leaves
5 cloves garlic, peeled
1 whole chicken
Salt and freshly ground pepper
1 litre milk
2 small carrots, chopped
5 spring onions, chopped
1 bunch fresh marjoram
100 ml fresh cream
1–2 rolls ready-made puff pastry
1 egg white

Add the butter, sage, basil and garlic to a stovetop-to-oven casserole dish. When the butter has melted, add the whole chicken and brown it as best you can on the outside. Season with salt and pepper. Once browned, add the milk, pop the lid on and allow to simmer over low heat for about 1 hour, turning the chicken after 30 minutes. When the chicken pulls easily from the bone, remove it from the casserole dish and set aside to cool in a dish large enough to catch all the juices.

Turn up the heat under the casserole dish and give everything in the pot a good stir, being sure to scrape up all those sticky bits from the bottom. Toss in the carrots, spring onions and marjoram, turn down the heat and simmer for 10 minutes.

Once the chicken has cooled enough to handle, pull off all the meat, rip into little bits and toss back into the casserole dish. Don't cut up the chicken … rip it up, it's much better. (Trust me.)

Add the juices/drippings from the cooled chicken and slowly stir in the cream over low heat. If you need to thicken the sauce a little, stir in 5 ml flour mashed together with 5 ml butter. Let it bubble gently for another 10 minutes and then remove from the heat.

Preheat the oven to 200 °C. Line a pie dish (or dishes) with puff pastry.* (Use your discretion as to how many rolls of pastry you will need.)

Scoop the chicken mixture into the pre-prepared pie dish. Cover the filling with a pastry lid and pierce a few holes in the lid with a fork to allow steam to escape. Brush a thin layer of egg white over the top and bake in the oven for 20 minutes, or until the top is golden brown.

Serve with buttery mash and one of your famous smiles. Beautiful!

* If you plan to freeze the pies for later use, be sure to allow the chicken filling to cool completely before filling the pie, then top and baste as normal. Wrap in a freezer bag and pop into the freezer. You can take them out and cook from frozen when you need them.

Sunday roasted and brined chicken

This is a real family favourite. I often use this method with our Christmas turkey, but a roast chicken is also fantastic prepared this way and it is made extra juicy by brining the bird overnight before roasting it very slowly at a very low temperature.

Brining is a great technique for keeping moisture in food and it is really easy to do. A little planning, yet minimal effort will guarantee a juicy, succulent and crisp bird every time.

BRINE
300 g salt
5 litres water
1 handful fresh thyme
1 handful fresh rosemary
25 g freshly ground black pepper
25 g mustard seeds
100 g brown sugar (optional)
2 bay leaves
5 cloves garlic, peeled

CHICKEN
1 whole chicken (1.5–2 kg)
1 lemon
A few sprigs fresh rosemary and thyme
Olive oil
50 g unsalted butter
60 ml white wine
A few sprigs fresh thyme, tarragon and sage
100 ml chicken stock
5 ml mustard powder

Make the brine first. Dissolve the salt in the water and then add the remaining brine ingredients. Set aside.

Remove the innards from the chicken and rinse the bird. Pat dry with paper towel and then place it in a clean container. Prick numerous little holes all over the bird with a sharp fork or toothpick to allow the brine to absorb more readily. Pour the brine over the chicken, ensuring that it is completely submerged. Cover the container and refrigerate overnight.

Remove the chicken from the liquid and dry well with paper towel. Discard the brine and set the chicken aside until it has reached room temperature.

Preheat the oven to 100 °C.

Cut the lemon in half and then place it in the cavity of the bird with the thyme and rosemary sprigs. Rub some oil onto the skin and truss the bird to stop the lemon and herbs from falling out.

Place the chicken on a rack in a roasting tray, cover and place in the oven. Roast the chicken until the legs feel like they will easily come off the bone when pulled, 3–4 hours.

Remove the chicken from the oven and set aside to rest for 45 minutes. Turn the oven temperature to the max.

In the meantime, melt the butter in a pan and add 30 ml wine and a few sprigs of thyme, tarragon and sage. Bring to the boil gently then remove the pan from the heat and use this herby butter to baste the chicken before and during browning.

Once the bird has rested, put the chicken back in the roasting tray and return it to the oven for approximately 10 minutes, or until golden brown, basting along the way and taking care that the skin doesn't burn. Once the bird is golden and crisp, remove from the oven and place on a cooling rack.

When the chicken has been browned and removed from the roasting tray, place the tray containing the juices on the hob over a medium-high heat. Add the remaining white wine and scrape and stir to deglaze the pan. Add the chicken stock and mustard powder and cook until reduced to a gravy. Strain into a gravy boat and season with salt and pepper to taste.

Serve with magic potatoes (see page 128) and a heap of roasted veg, and then brace yourself: You are about to become a kitchen legend.

SERVES 4–6

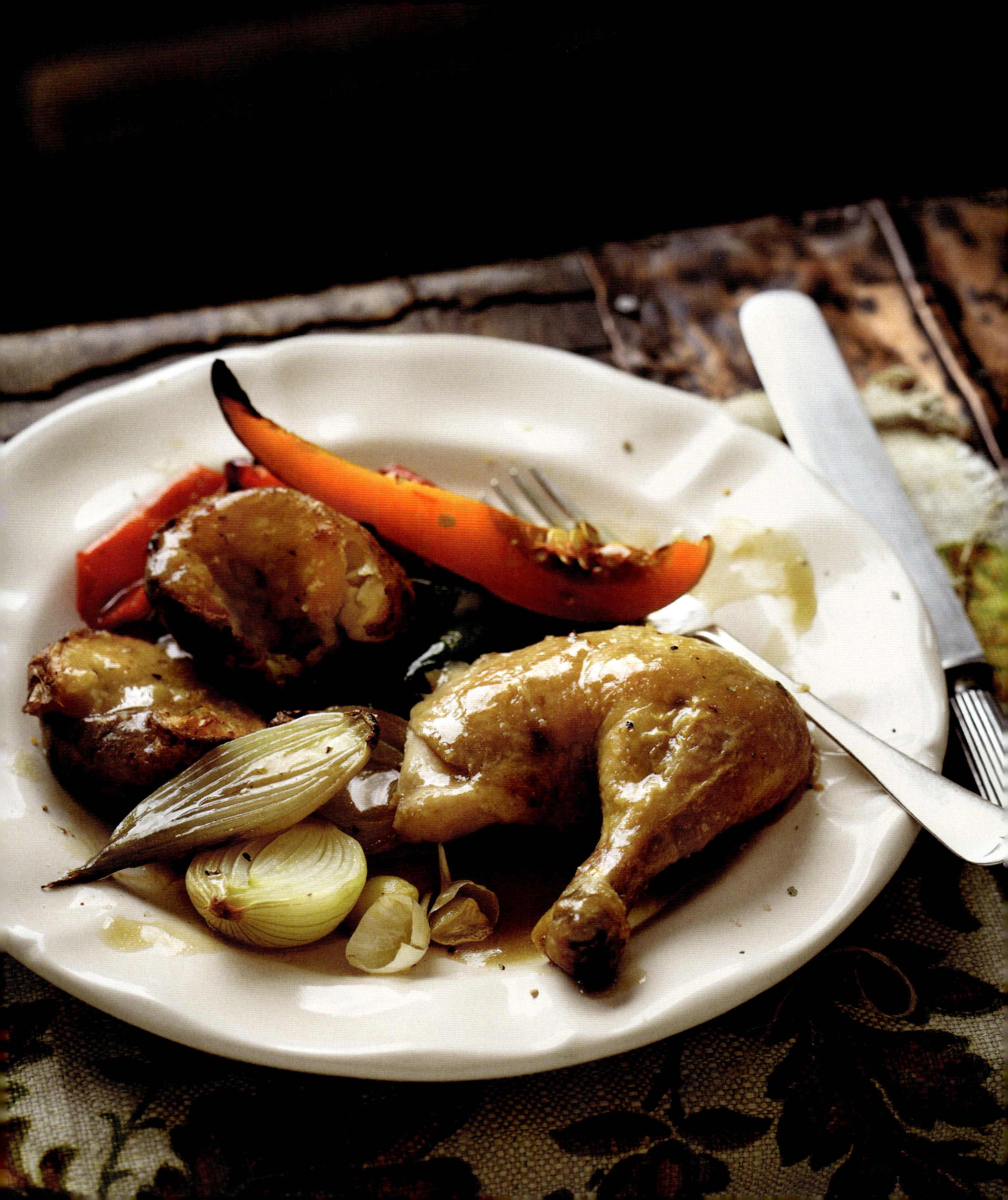

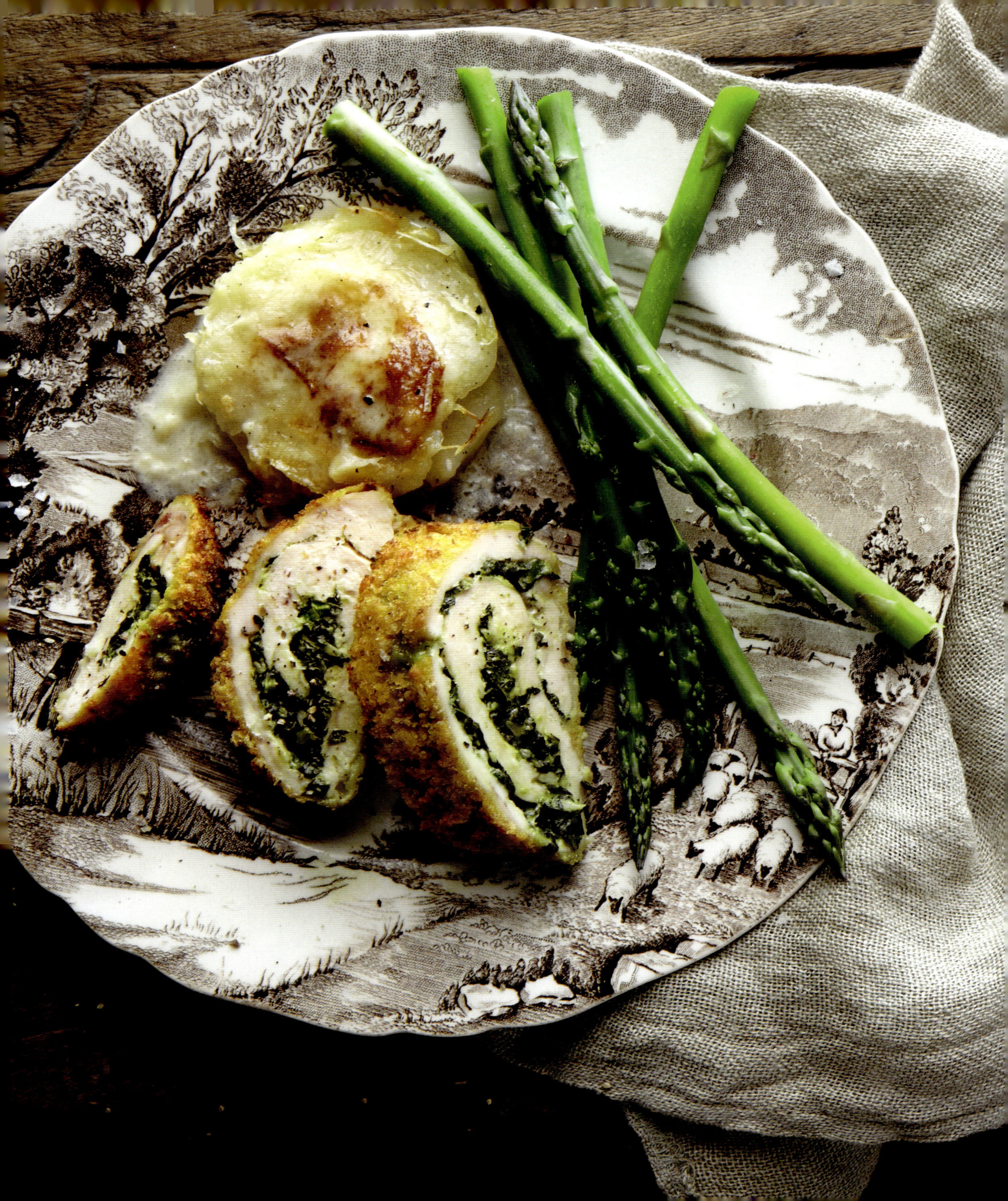

Chicken breast roulade with fresh morogo and feta

I serve this in the restaurant when the marog is in season. Morogo (amaranth) is a type of wild African spinach and grows almost anywhere in southern Africa. It is an ancient crop that is highly nutritious and full of flavour. It is very easy to cook and the seeds can even be ground into a high-protein flour. I tend to treat morogo the same as I do my spinach. If you can't find any morogo, you can substitute spinach or Swiss chard.

For this dish you will need large free-range chicken breasts, and each breast should be enough to feed two people. This is a lot easier to do than it looks, so give it a go and you may well surprise yourself and your friends.

---

2 large skinless chicken breast fillets
2 handfuls morogo, washed and finely chopped (it cooks down a lot so don't stress if it looks like too much initially)
150 g feta cheese, crumbled
Salt and freshly ground pepper
125 ml cake flour
2 eggs, beaten
200 g fresh breadcrumbs
Olive oil

Using a meat mallet or rolling pin, pound the breasts between two pieces of greaseproof paper until they are flat (1–1.5 cm thick). Set aside.

Heat a pan and wilt the morogo with a splash of water for about 3 minutes. Toss in the feta and heat for another 2 minutes. You don't really want to cook it, you just want to soften the feta and get the morogo down to a smaller batch of usable filling. Season to taste and set aside to cool.

Place a layer of the cooled morogo mixture onto the flattened breasts and roll them into a tight bundle resembling a Swiss roll. Dust with flour. Refrigerate for 30 minutes to set. Once set, gently roll in the beaten egg and then in the crumbs. Return to the fridge to settle. (Wrap them in plastic wrap if you need to.)

When ready to cook, pop the breasts onto a baking tray, drizzle with olive oil and bake in a preheated oven at 180 °C for 20 minutes, or until golden brown and firm to the touch. Remove from the oven and leave to rest for 5 minutes.

Cut crossways into 1.5 cm-thick slices and serve with crisp green veg and mini potato bakes (see page 126). Lekker!

SERVES 2–4

Wholegrain and herbed pancakes with creamy sage chicken filling

Whenever it gets cold and rainy, my family wants pancakes. Lots of pancakes. Apart from the traditional cinnamon and sugar ones, I also like to get creative and try turning them into a wholesome and tasty meal that is also fun and can involve everyone in the preparation. The kids love helping and it definitely helps to cure cabin fever.

We make up all sorts of interesting fillings, but this chicken one is definitely a firm favourite.

PANCAKES
3 eggs
125 g cake flour
125 g good wholewheat flour
40 ml chopped fresh dill
20 ml finely chopped fresh tarragon
40 ml finely chopped spring onions
5 ml castor sugar
5 ml salt
125 ml milk
125 ml fresh cream
50 ml brandy (optional)
25 ml water
Olive oil

CREAMY SAGE CHICKEN FILLING
Olive oil
15 ml thick soy sauce
4 skinless chicken breast fillets, patted dry
½ onion, finely chopped
2 cloves garlic, finely chopped
5 ml turmeric
4 fresh sage leaves, finely chopped
250 ml thick fresh cream
100 g grated Gouda cheese
Salt and freshly ground pepper

To make the pancakes, whisk the eggs well. Mix the cake flour, wholewheat flour, herbs and spring onions together in a separate bowl. Add the sugar and the salt to the herb mix.

Add the milk, cream and brandy to the eggs. Gradually add the herb mix and stir until thick and lump free. Add water until the mixture has the consistency of fairly thick cream. Set aside for 10 minutes to settle.

To cook the pancakes, heat a small frying pan over medium heat and wipe a thin layer of olive oil onto the base. Stir 15 ml olive oil into the batter (this prevents the batter from sticking to the pan).

Place 15 ml of the batter into the pan and swirl around until the base is covered in a thin layer of batter. Cook until it starts to bubble and there are brown bubbles on the underside of the pancake (you need to lift an edge with an egg lifter to take a peek). If ready, flip the pancake and cook until done. Remove and repeat until all the batter is finished. Stack the pancakes on top of one another and set aside in the warmer drawer in a covered dish to prevent them from drying out.

To make the filling, heat a little olive oil in a heavy-based pan. Rub soy sauce over the chicken while the pan is warming up. Place the whole breasts into the hot pan and do not turn them until they are golden brown underneath (in other words, try not to turn them too much, just let them cook through on each side until golden brown). Remove from the pan and set aside to cool.

Reduce the heat to medium and, using the same pan, add the onion, garlic, turmeric and sage. Sweat off for 5 minutes until soft.

In the meantime, tear up the chicken breasts (do not cut them with a knife, use your fingers – kids love to do this) into smallish shreds. Return the chicken to the pan and turn the heat right down, giving everything a good stir. Add the cream very slowly, and then stir in the cheese and allow the whole lot to simmer very gently for 5 minutes. Do not let it boil as the cream will separate. You just want everything to heat through. Season to taste.

Fill the pancakes with the mixture and enjoy with the whole family while staring out at the lovely rain and trying to count the drops.

THE RECIPE MAKES ENOUGH FOR 6–10 THIN, SIDE PLATE-SIZED PANCAKES (double up if you want more)

Hole chicken

This may seem like a crazy concept, but cooking underground goes back thousands of years. This recipe is handy if you are camping or out in the veld for a picnic and it is super low maintenance. Everyone can help with the fire, digging the hole and that sort of thing, but once the chicken is in the hole you can forget about it for a few hours and when you come back later, lunch or dinner will be ready.

---

1 large whole free-range chicken or Cornish hen
1 orange, quartered
1 onion, quartered
1 stalk celery, roughly chopped, with leaves
2 red chillies
2 green chillies
4 cloves garlic, chopped
150 ml olive oil

SALT CRUST DOUGH
750 ml bread flour
15 ml fine salt
300 ml water

Stuff the cavity of the chicken with the orange, onion, celery, chillies and half the garlic. Rub the outer skin with olive oil and the remaining garlic. Leave to marinate for 24 hours to let the flavours infuse.

To make the dough, mix the flour and salt together. Slowly add the water until the texture is dryish yet springy. Knead until smooth. Cover and leave.

When the chicken has marinated, roll out the salt crust dough until it is big enough to cover the whole bird. Place the bird on top and fold the dough upwards, so it resembles a bag. Dip your fingers in water and squeeze the top together to make sure it is firmly sealed.

Now dig a hole in the ground!

Line the hole with rocks. Make a big fire in the hole and allow it to burn down to coals. Place the wrapped chicken on a baking tray and place some stones or bricks around the tray (high enough to support a corrugated sheet without touching the chicken). Top with a sheet of corrugated iron or sheet metal. Weigh down with a few rocks and cover the sheet with coals and wood and let the chicken cook in the ground for approximately 3 hours. During this time check on the coals to ensure they are still hot.

After 3 hours lift the chicken out of the ground. The dough will have hardened. Crack it open with a panga or a large knife. The chicken will be moist and cooked.

Enjoy!

1 CHICKEN WILL EASILY FEED 5–6 PEOPLE

Lemon and thyme chicken burgers

These are great for a healthy, wholesome burger lunch or supper. When the kids feel like fast food, give them these instead. You can cheat by buying chicken mince or breasts from your butcher to save time. I find, though, that just using breast meat can leave the patties a little dry so I prefer to use a mixture of all the chicken cuts to ensure a succulent, juicy patty. Experiment and see what works best for you. They freeze very well so you can store any extras for another meal.

1 whole chicken
Zest of 1 lemon
4 large sprigs fresh thyme
20 ml salt
10 ml ground black pepper
1 egg
125 ml cake flour
Olive oil
Salad leaves or rocket

Debone the chicken and cut the meat into 5 cm cubes. Add the lemon zest, thyme and seasoning, mix thoroughly and refrigerate overnight.

Mince the chicken mixture using a medium mincing blade. Add the egg, and then add flour, a little bit at a time, until you get the consistency of meatballs.

Shape the mixture into patties and refrigerate for 1 hour. Heat a little olive oil and fry the patties until golden and delicious.

Serve on a toasty bun with salad leaves and sweet chilli sauce and potato wedges on the side.

Badabingbadaboom! The most awesome slow food chicken burgers ever!

VARIATION

Mix grated Parmesan and brown breadcrumbs together or use uncooked couscous to make a crunchy coating for the patties.
Coat with egg and crumb the patties just before frying.

MAKES ABOUT 12 GOOD-SIZED PATTIES

FREE-RANGE CHICKEN 79

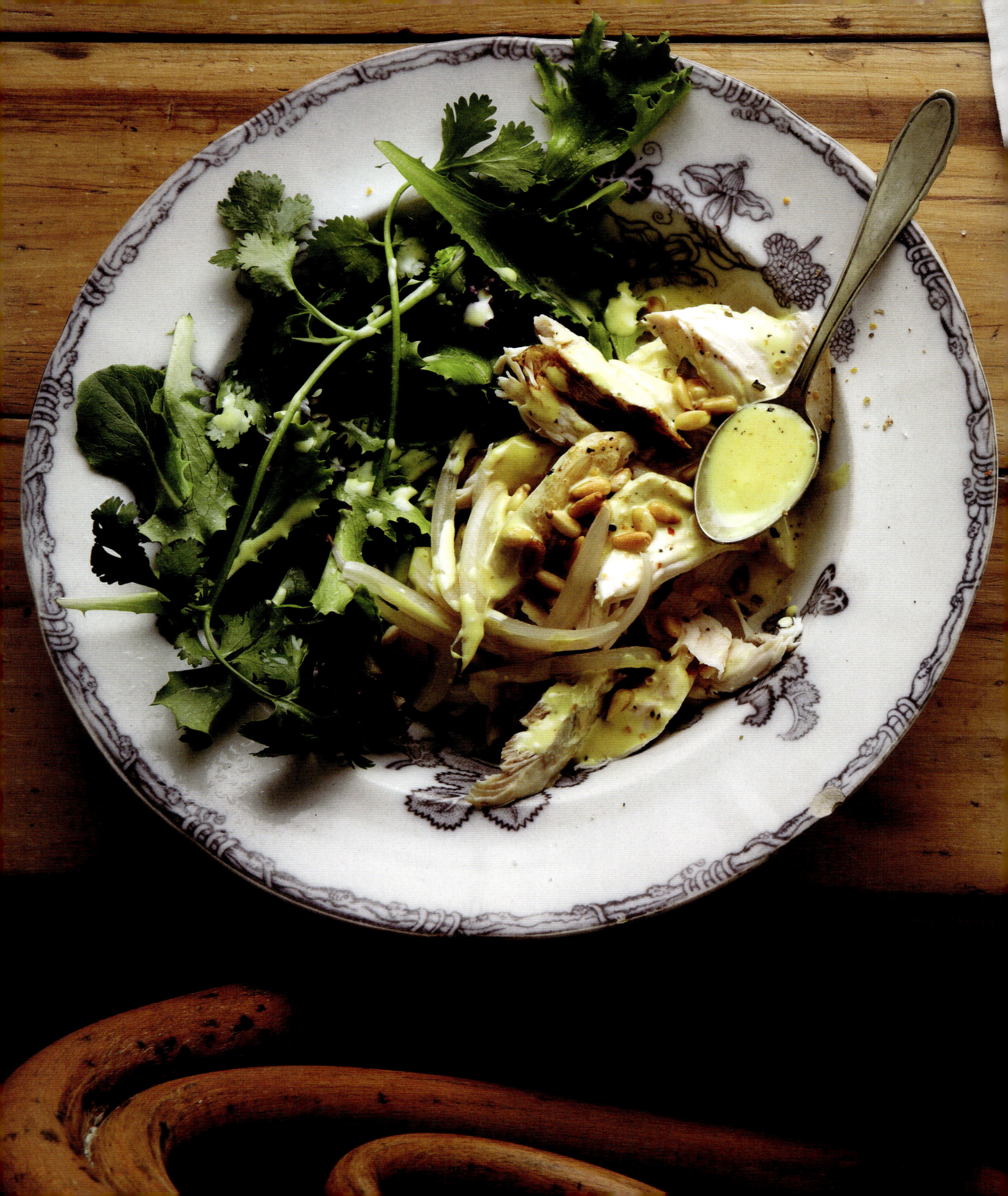

Chicken curry salad

This easy summer salad is a great way to use up leftover chicken from a braai.* I will, however, often braai chicken pieces specifically for that lekker smoky braai taste it gives the meat.

---

125 g honey
45 ml chutney
25 ml mild and spicy curry powder
125 ml white wine
300 ml mayonnaise
1 cooked chicken (or leftover chicken pieces), deboned and flaked
Pine nuts (optional)
1 onion, sliced and sweated off

Heat the honey, chutney and curry powder together over low heat for 20 minutes. Remove from the heat and cool completely.

Add the wine, and then fold in the mayonnaise. Thin with more wine if necessary. Allow the chicken to cool and then mix it into the sauce. Refrigerate.

I like to serve this on frilly lettuce leaves with a sprinkling of pine nuts and the sweated onion on top.

* You can even use this as a sandwich filling. My editor thinks it sounds delicious, and so do I.

SERVES 4–6

© Gordon Wright

Venison, Furred and Fowl

This section, then, is the true heart and soul of this book. It is a tribute to my absolute passion for hunting and working with venison, the king of meats.

As I write this page it is winter and we're slap bang in the middle of the hunting season. We're experiencing a particularly cold winter, so we've been indulging in lots of comfort food, stews, soups and, of course, curries. All made from delectable venison.

When I talk about venison, I refer to all wild game animals and include game birds and smaller critters, such as hare and rabbit. Wild game is one of the healthiest meats available and you don't really get much that is more free-range and organic than that.

I want to impress upon you all, my dear reader, hunter and cook, how important it is to give your quarry the respect and dignity it deserves, from the veld all the way to your fork, to ensure a perfect end result to your venison dishes.

Game animals are generally very highly strung and suffer stress easily due to the fact that in the wild they have to contend with predators and threats to their survival on a constant basis. The slightest threat can set off their fight or flight reflex.

Domestic livestock generally have very few predators and are used to the presence of humans, so this reflex is well inhibited and thus seldom activated.

The first thing that happens when a wild animal is startled is a massive release of adrenaline, which is like a super, natural steroid that is pumped into all the critical areas and muscles of the body to enable the animal to see, hear and move incredibly well and quickly and get the heck out of harms way as soon as possible. This process is what is commonly known as the fight or flight reflex.

This reflex is an anaerobic process, which means that the muscles do not rely on oxygen to perform optimally. The muscle cells must then rely on other reactions that do not require oxygen to fuel muscle contraction, which in turn produces waste molecules, such as lactic acid, that can impair muscle contractions. We generally call this deterioration in performance fatigue. In wild game this sort of stress translates into tough and gamey meat. Not good.

But enough with the biology lesson, the key thing you need to know here is that when hunting or working with venison, it is very important that the quarry was in as stress free a condition as possible when it breathed its last.

© Rose Wright

If you are doing the hunting yourself, you need to hunt as ethically and humanely as possible to ensure a quick and painless end. Should you not be the hunting type but are still game for game, make sure, when buying venison, that you know how it was hunted. Badly shot or wounded game meat should be avoided at all costs and it is imperative that it should've been hung for at least 7 days at 4 °C.

The older generation tended to over marinate their venison. Their hunting methods were different too, and when a herd of springbok got chased around all day this influenced the flavour of the meat, i.e. tough and gamey, and therefore the method of preparation. A lot of vinegar and marinades were used to try to get rid of the gamey flavour and reduce the toughness (no convenient fridges to hang the meat in those days). Well-hunted and hung venison is soft, delicate and full of flavour and needs little to no marinating.

My advice to anyone preparing venison is this: if you know it was well hunted, treat it similarly to a good cut of beef. Keep the flavours simple and basic.

'Vegetarian' is an old tribal word for 'bad hunter' – Anon.

A HUNTER'S PRAYER
(to the slain animal's spirit)

Life is a circle. At first, we do not exist in this world. Then we are born, grow, and thus live. Then after a while, when we must relinquish our existence in this world, the circle is complete. Some circles are very small, others much larger. We do not much control where the circle starts or ends. But within this circle, we are players whose performance is a balance of conscious and unconscious choices; influences from that which is imprinted within our species and that which is imposed from without.

As such, I have not chosen to be predator any more than you have chosen to be prey. The circle of life demands that there be both. I accept that as predator, I have the awesome responsibility of being swift and sure, for carelessness may cause you suffering, and that I cannot bear. Yet, because I am sometimes less than I can be, I will cause suffering. May I be thus judged by the sincerity of my intentions, and the purity of my heart, and when it is deserved, may I be forgiven.

I celebrate the way you lived, I wish I could live my life as well. Your courage and love of life was not a minor thing. Therefore, it is now with both sorrow and reverence that I now thank you, noble creature, for giving your life, and I honour your life by pledging that through your death will come sustenance for renewed life. Now that your spirit has been set free, it can go where it will.

However, if you think I am worthy, perhaps you will honour me by allowing your spirit to come into my heart where it can live within me and be my counsel. And when life comes full circle for me, may both of our spirits be set free in a better place –

Where the 'lion can lay with the lamb' and we will feel sorrow and fear no more.
JDG 1999

Grey-winged partridge breasts with barley and baby peas

One of my good mates, Conrad Kasperski, runs Wingshooting Africa Safaris out of Graaff-Reinet and is one of the legends of the wingshooting fraternity. When we hunt grey-winged partridge (or bergpatrys *as it is known in these parts, although officially it is the grey-winged francolin), it is always a tough mission, but the rewards are well worth the effort and I get to enjoy a great day out in the fresh air and the mountains. Conrad enjoys the camaraderie of the hunt as much as he does being out with his dogs, and he always ensures that I make a scrummy veld cook-up in some beautiful lunchtime location he has scouted out.*

Barley is a bit of a forgotten ingredient in modern cooking but it's fantastic in stews and soups. The partridge breast has a gentle flavour, but you can also use quail or another similar game bird.

I really don't remember who I got this recipe from but have been using it for ages, so I apologise in advance if it was you who gave the idea to me and I have not given you the due credit.

---

120 g pearled barley
Olive oil
1 red onion, finely chopped
Sea salt and freshly ground black pepper
2 cups good chicken or vegetable stock
20 ml cake flour
30 ml butter
150 g baby peas
100 g thick bacon or pancetta, rind removed, diced
4 partridge breasts, washed and patted dry
A few sprigs fresh thyme, leaves picked and chopped
1 handful frilly lettuce, washed and dried
1 handful rocket, washed and dried

Cook the pearled barley in boiling, salted water for about 50 minutes, or until tender. Drain and leave to steam dry.

Heat a glug of olive oil in a frying pan and add the onion and a pinch of salt. Sweat on a low heat for about 5 minutes, or until the onion is translucent and soft. Add the barley. Cover with the stock and bring to the boil. Simmer for 10 minutes, stirring every now and then.

Mash the flour and butter together with a fork until you have a paste. Stir half of the paste into the barley and continue to simmer until the liquid begins to thicken. If, after 5 minutes, it's not thick enough, add some more of the paste. What you want to achieve is a silky smooth broth. Now add the peas and continue to simmer for another 10 minutes, adding a little extra stock if it gets too dry.

Heat some more olive oil in another frying pan. Add the bacon bits and fry and shake them about until they're lightly golden.

Meanwhile, lay out the partridge breasts and sprinkle with the chopped thyme and a good pinch of seasoning. Press the thyme onto both sides of the breasts.

When the bacon is crisp, push it to one side of the pan. Place the breasts in the pan, skin side up. Cook for 4 minutes, then turn and cook the other side for 1 minute to crisp the skin. You can cook them for longer if you like your meat well done.

When the breasts are done, taste the barley broth and adjust the seasoning. Stir in the lettuce and rocket – they only need a minute or so to cook.

Serve the barley, peas and lettuce with the partridge breasts on top and sprinkle with the bacon pieces. Spoon the broth over the top.

SERVES 2

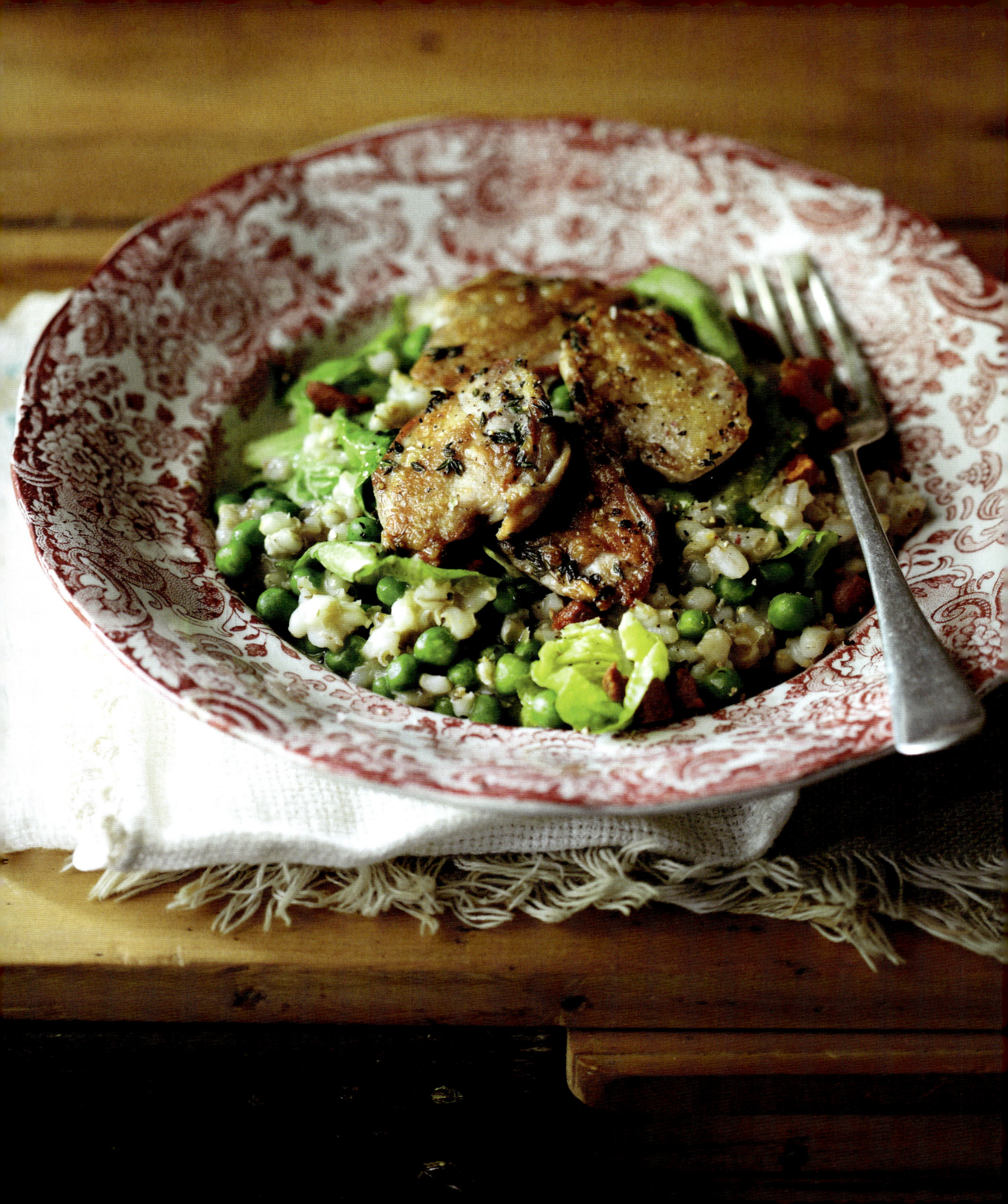

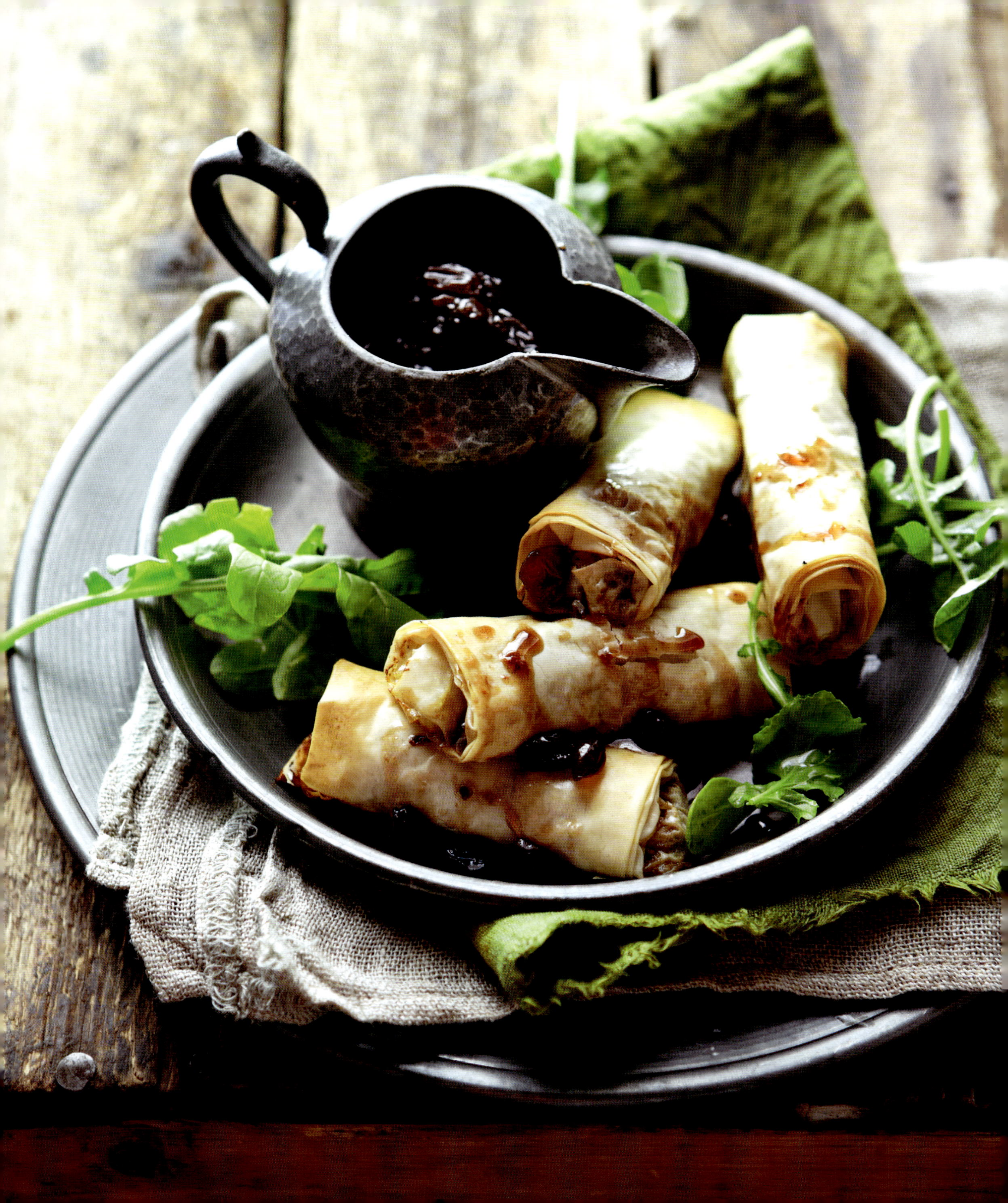

Baked wild hare spring rolls with raisin and Muscadel sauce

Wild hare and rabbit have been a staple part of the diet of most of the Karoo population since day one and only in the past 50 years or so has it fallen from favour due to the abundance of lamb, beef and the like. It remains, however, a fabulous source of lean, tasty and healthy protein that is sadly underrated by many South Africans. Whenever I hunt, I always see plenty of spring and scrub-type hares about and always bag a few for the pot. I love experimenting with the flavours and this recipe has become one of my signature dishes at the restaurant. I have yet to meet someone who is not bowled over by it. So be a brave bunny and try it!

---

1 cleaned whole hare or rabbit
Salt and freshly ground black pepper
1 bottle (750 ml) good-quality white wine (ideally the same wine you will be drinking with the meal)
3 large sprigs fresh rosemary
Olive oil
2 onions, finely chopped
5 cloves fresh garlic, finely chopped
25 g fresh thyme
50 g freshly chopped rosemary
250 ml fresh cream
1 bunch spring onions, chopped
Phyllo pastry sheets
25 ml melted butter
Rocket, for serving

RAISIN AND MUSCADEL SAUCE
1 packet (250 g) raisins
½ bottle (375 ml) red Muscadel or a suitable fortified sweet wine

Prepare the sauce first. Soak the raisins in Muscadel overnight until the raisins are soft and swollen. Pour the whole lot into a saucepan and bring to the boil. Reduce the heat and simmer until reduced by a third. Remove from the heat and leave to cool.

Preheat the oven to 180 °C.

To prepare the hare, place the whole hare, seasoned with salt and pepper, in a large roasting dish. Add the wine and rosemary sprigs, pop the lid on and roast in the oven for 1½ hours, or until the meat is tender and falling off the bone. Once done, set aside and allow to cool.

Once cool, remove the meat from the bone and chop finely (retain pan juices for later).

Heat a glug of olive oil in a fairly deep saucepan, add the onions and sweat off. Add the garlic, chopped up hare, thyme and chopped rosemary. Reduce the heat and simmer for 3 minutes, stirring continuously.

Stir in the cream and some of the pan juices – do not boil. Allow to simmer gently with the lid on for 10 minutes. (The mixture should be juicy and moist and not too wet and runny.) Stir in the spring onions and remove from the heat immediately. Set aside to cool.

Using a sharp knife, cut a sheet of phyllo pastry into three equal strips. Brush along the top edge with melted butter. Place a tablespoon of hare filling at the bottom of each sheet and roll into a spring roll. Repeat with the rest of the phyllo and filling.

Brush the outside of the spring rolls with melted butter and bake at 180 °C for 10 minutes, or until golden brown.

To serve, place a handful of fresh rocket on each plate and drizzle over a tablespoon of raisin sauce. Place a hot spring roll on top. Serve immediately with a fruity Sauvignon Blanc or a dry Rosé.

MAKES 10–15 SPRING ROLLS

The ultimate hunter's stew with wild mushrooms and brown rice

This is the most exciting dish I think I have ever created. It combines all the best game meats into one creamy, mushroomy and most decadent of stews. It has all my favourite game meats in it: kudu, springbok, mountain reedbuck as well as rabbit and guinea fowl.

I am also wild about mushrooms so I've thrown in a whole heap of different, strong-flavoured mushies as well as loads of garlic, rosemary and piles of other herbs. This recipe is supposed to be a celebration of all things game so you can substitute any of the meats with your favourites.

---

750 g brown rice
Olive oil
1 red onion, roughly chopped
4 cloves garlic, roughly chopped
1 thick piece ginger, finely chopped
500 g kudu shanks, sawn into pieces
500 g springbok shanks, sawn into pieces
500 g mountain reedbuck shanks, sawn into pieces
1 whole rabbit or hare, deboned and cut into cubes
1 whole guinea fowl, deboned and cut into cubes
Salt and freshly ground black pepper
15 ml paprika
1 handful finely chopped fresh rosemary, flat-leaf parsley, oregano and thyme
Knob of butter
125 ml brandy
150 ml sour cream
Zest of ½ lemon
500 g carrots, green beans, courgettes and green asparagus, roughly chopped
250 g assorted strong-flavoured wild mushrooms, thickly sliced (you can get the assorted packs at most good food stores)

Preheat the oven to 180 °C.

Prepare the brown rice as per the package instructions.

Heat a little olive oil in a large stovetop-to-oven casserole and sweat the onion, garlic and ginger until soft. Remove from the dish and set aside.

Rub all the meat with salt, pepper and paprika. Add another glug of oil to the casserole and brown the meat in batches. Return the garlic, onion and ginger to the dish along with the herbs and butter.

Toss in the brandy and flambé. (Watch your eyebrows!) The flambéing really adds a complexity of flavour. Give it a good stir and when the flames die out stir in three-quarters of the sour cream and the lemon zest. Put the lid on and pop into the oven for 1 hour.

Add the veg, except the asparagus, and cook for a further 30 minutes.

Toss in the mushrooms and asparagus, stirring carefully so as not to break up the other veg. Cook for a further 20 minutes. The mushrooms and asparagus should be crunchy and full of flavour while the rest should be soft, tender and delicious.

Serve over the brown rice with a dollop of sour cream and sprinkle of chopped flat-leaf parsley. A good Cabernet Sauvignon should round this dish off nicely.

SERVES 5–7

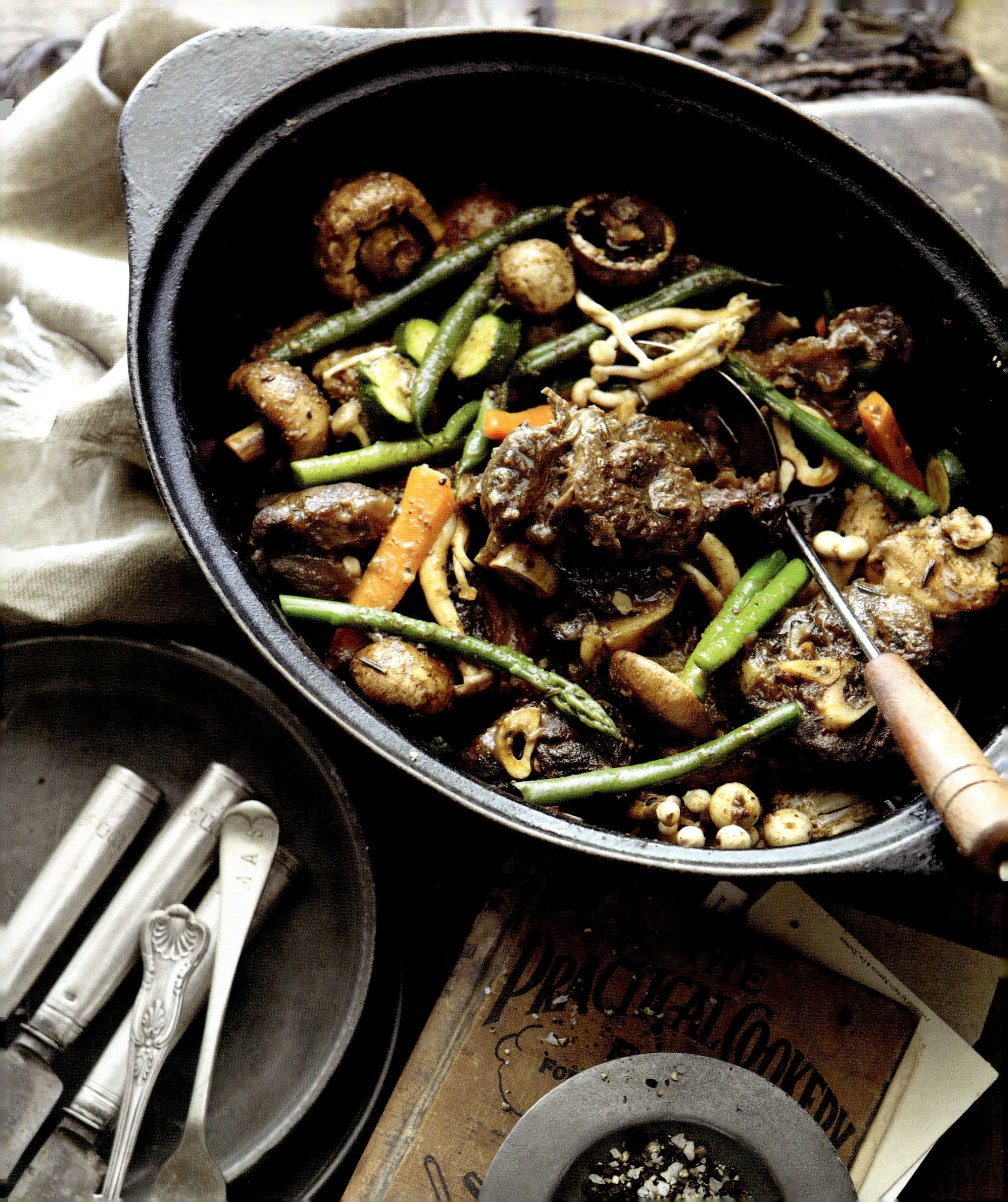
THE
PRACTICAL

Classic Karoo roasted shoulder of springbok with homemade smoked bacon

This is one of my all-time favourites. The prep is very quick and simple and the slow-roasting results in meltingly soft venison shoulder, juicy and falling off the bone.

I love to use a smallish shoulder like springbok or mountain reedbuck and leave the shank on as this adds a whole new dimension to the roast. The secret to this roast is to keep the lid on – tight as can be – throughout the cooking process. I bang all the ingredients into the roasting dish and then make a sticky dough by mixing some flour and water, which I use to seal around the rim of the dish. When I put the lid on it forms an airtight seal so that nothing can escape. I put it into a very hot oven (around 280 °C or as close as your oven can get to that, if you are my editor) for 10 minutes to get the whole process going and then turn the heat right down to 150 °C for another 2 hours. The end result is a flavoursome, soft and unbelievably succulent roast with the most incredible pan juices to use as a base for your gravy. Are you drooling yet?

---

1 venison shoulder roast, shank still attached
Olive oil
Salt and freshly ground pepper
1 bottle (750 ml) good-quality white wine (half for you and half for the roast)
10 cloves garlic, peeled
1 large thumb-sized piece fresh ginger, cut into chunks
1 handful fresh rosemary sprigs
100 g thickly sliced homemade bacon (see recipe on page 114, or use thickly sliced shop-bought bacon)
30 ml smooth apricot jam or quince jelly

Preheat the oven to 280 °C, or as near as dammit!

Rub the roast with olive oil, salt and pepper. Pour the wine into the roasting dish so that it is about 5 cm deep. Add the garlic, ginger and rosemary to the wine and place the roast in the dish. Cover with rashers of bacon and seal the lid in place as described in the intro above.

Place in the hot oven for 10 minutes, then reduce the oven temperature to 150 °C and continue roasting for 2 hours. **Do not open the lid during this time!**

After 2 hours remove from the oven and check (be careful of the steam when opening the lid). You should be able to pull out the scapula (the thin flat bone at the end) quite easily. If not, close up and cook for longer. Once ready, remove the roast from the pan and set aside to rest.

Strain the pan juices through a sieve, pushing through all the goodness with a spoon. Return the juices to the pan with the apricot jam and bring to the boil whilst stirring and scraping all the sticky dark stuff off the bottom – lots of flavour here. Thicken if necessary and voilà! You have brilliant gravy to go with your roast.

SERVES 4–6

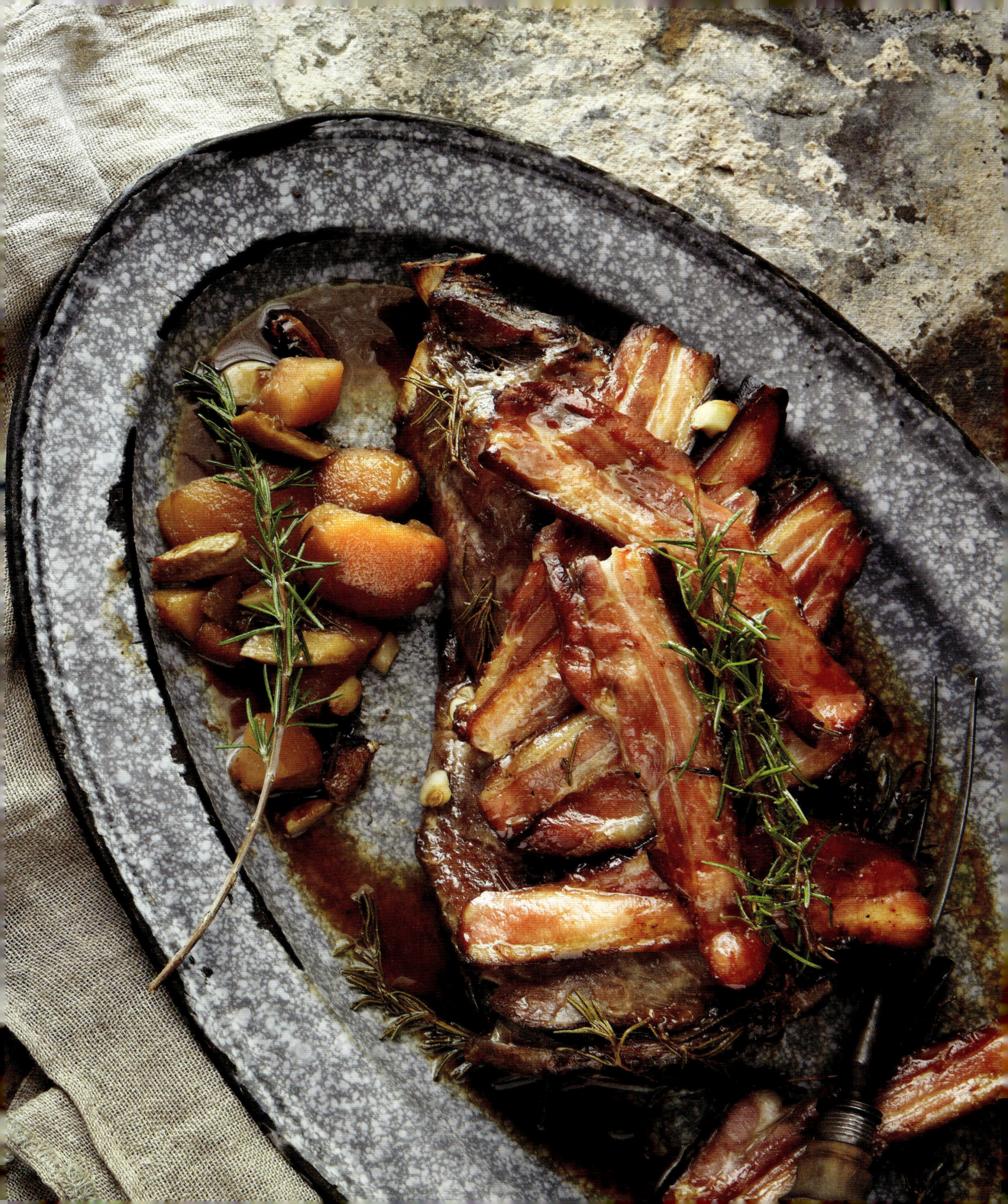

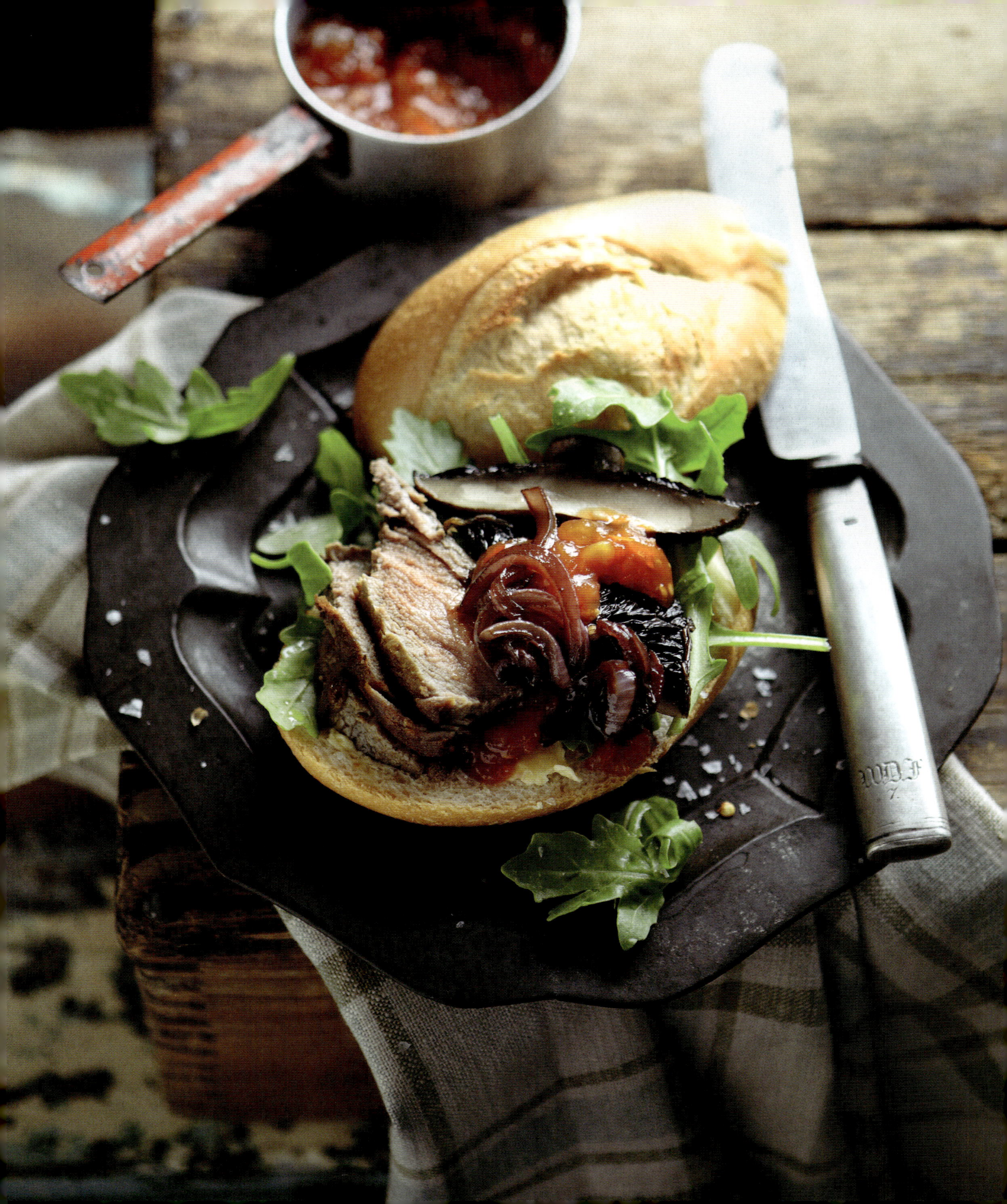

Nadia Kitching's awesome eland steak roll with mild chilli sauce and balsamic onions

Nadia and Shaun are two of our great mates. Shaun the gentle giant and Nadia, the kindest, most loving wife a guy could ask for, are such a good match. Nadia has Italian blood and Shaun is pure SA beef and they both love nothing better than cooking up a storm in their kitchen when they can.

Shaun loves hunting and the outdoors and they both love venison, so they came up with this great lunchtime dish. It's perfect for a summer's day or for when you have a big crowd to feed – everyone can muck in and help prepare and then make their own rolls around the table outside. You can grill the steak on the braai as well if you want.

Eland sirloin steak or fillet (actually, any good prime cut of venison will do)
Olive oil
Splash of Worcestershire sauce
2 cloves garlic, chopped
Crushed coriander seeds
Salt and freshly ground pepper
1 large brown mushroom per person
Fresh bread rolls
Rocket

MILD CHILLI SAUCE (PER PERSON)
½ large red onion, finely chopped
1 tomato, peeled and roughly chopped or 5 whole roma tomatoes
1 chilli, roughly chopped (deseed if you don't want too much fire)

BALSAMIC ONION (PER PERSON)
½ large red onion, sliced into rings
Balsamic vinegar
5 ml brown sugar

Marinate the steak/s in a little olive oil, Worcestershire sauce, half the garlic and the coriander seeds for about 30 minutes.

Make the chilli sauce while the meat is marinating. Heat a little olive oil and sweat the chopped onion and the rest of the garlic until soft. Add the chopped tomato and chilli, and simmer until it reduces to a thick sauce. Remove from the heat and set aside.

Preheat the oven to 180 °C.

Heat a thick-based griddle pan until smoking hot. Do not add oil or anything else yet.

Whilst the pan is heating, place the mushrooms onto a roasting tray and bake for 5 minutes. Switch off the oven and leave the mushrooms inside until ready to plate.

When the griddle pan is super-hot, smear the marinade on the steaks one last time and sear on all sides until medium-rare at most. Remove from the pan and allow to rest for 5 minutes.

While the steak is resting, heat a little olive oil in a pan and sweat off the onion rings until soft. Add the balsamic vinegar and brown sugar and reduce to form a sticky reduction.

Butter the rolls and add some rocket. Thinly slice the steak and place on top of the rocket. Season to taste with salt and pepper and add onion rings, sauce and sliced mushrooms.

Enjoy with a good glass of red to top it off.

SERVES 2–4 (depending on the size of the steak)

Easy as … baked guinea fowl samoosas with a mango and chilli relish

I love guinea fowl; I think it is one of the tastiest of the game birds and such a challenge to hunt. I came up with this recipe after an idea from my brother Bernard, who is a really good cook and loves being in the kitchen. He travels the world extensively on business and is always looking for and finding all sorts of interesting ingredients and recipes. It is such a treat to have dinner at his home when we get a chance (and it's good to have other people cooking for me for a change). I can't remember exactly what the original recipe was, but the mango chilli relish stood out for me and I had to try it with other things. I had been hunting guinea fowl the previous weekend and had been talking to the Indian lady at the spice shop down the road when the idea to do samoosas hit me. I know it is not a traditional Karoo dish, but it is so delicious I am sure you will forgive me. The combination of sweet and spicy goes so well with the guinea fowl, and the coriander gives everything a wonderful fresh complexity.

These samoosas make a great starter or are perfect for a summer's day or evening canapé. They can be prepared the day before, kept in the fridge and popped into the oven 10 minutes before serving. Easy as …

Olive oil
1 whole guinea fowl, cleaned, cut into pieces and patted dry with paper towel
Salt and freshly ground black pepper
1 bottle (750 ml) good-quality white wine (ideally the same wine you will be drinking with the meal)
3 large sprigs fresh rosemary
1 orange, quartered
2 onions, finely chopped
5 cloves garlic, finely chopped
50 g dried cranberries
175 ml fresh cream
50 g fresh rosemary, chopped
1 bunch spring onions
Phyllo pastry sheets
25 ml melted butter
Rocket, for serving

MANGO AND CHILLI RELISH
5 fresh red chillies, deseeded and chopped
1 handful fresh coriander
1 ripe mango, peeled and finely chopped
1 fresh lime

Make the relish first. Gently fold the chillies and coriander into the mango, making sure not to mash the mango. Add a squeeze of lime juice and gently mix once more. Refrigerate until needed.

Preheat the oven to 180 °C.

To prepare the guinea fowl, heat a little olive oil in a stovetop-to-oven casserole dish. Season the pieces of guinea fowl with salt and pepper, and brown lightly. Cover with wine and add the rosemary sprigs and orange. Cover with the lid and roast for 1½ hours, or until the meat is tender and falling off the bone. Once done, allow to cool.

Remove the meat from the bones and chop finely (retain pan juices for later). Clean the saucepan and heat a glug of olive oil. Add the onions and sweat off. Add the garlic and chopped guinea fowl, reduce the heat and simmer for 3 minutes, stirring continuously. Stir in the cranberries, cream, rosemary and pan juices, as necessary, and simmer with the lid on for 10 minutes. (Do not allow to boil, as the cream will separate!) The mixture should not be too wet and sauce-like but rather juicy and moist. Stir in the spring onions and remove from the heat immediately. Set aside to cool.

Using a sharp knife, cut a sheet of phyllo pastry into three equal strips. Brush along the top edge with melted butter. Place a tablespoon of guinea fowl filling at the bottom of each sheet and fold into a mini samoosa. Repeat with the rest of the phyllo and filling. Brush the outside of the samoosas with butter and bake at 180 °C for 10 minutes, or until golden brown.

To serve, place a handful of fresh rocket on each plate and add a spoonful of relish. Place the samoosas on top. Serve immediately with a crisp, fruity Chenin Blanc or a dry Rosé. Lovely!

MAKES 10–15 SAMOOSAS

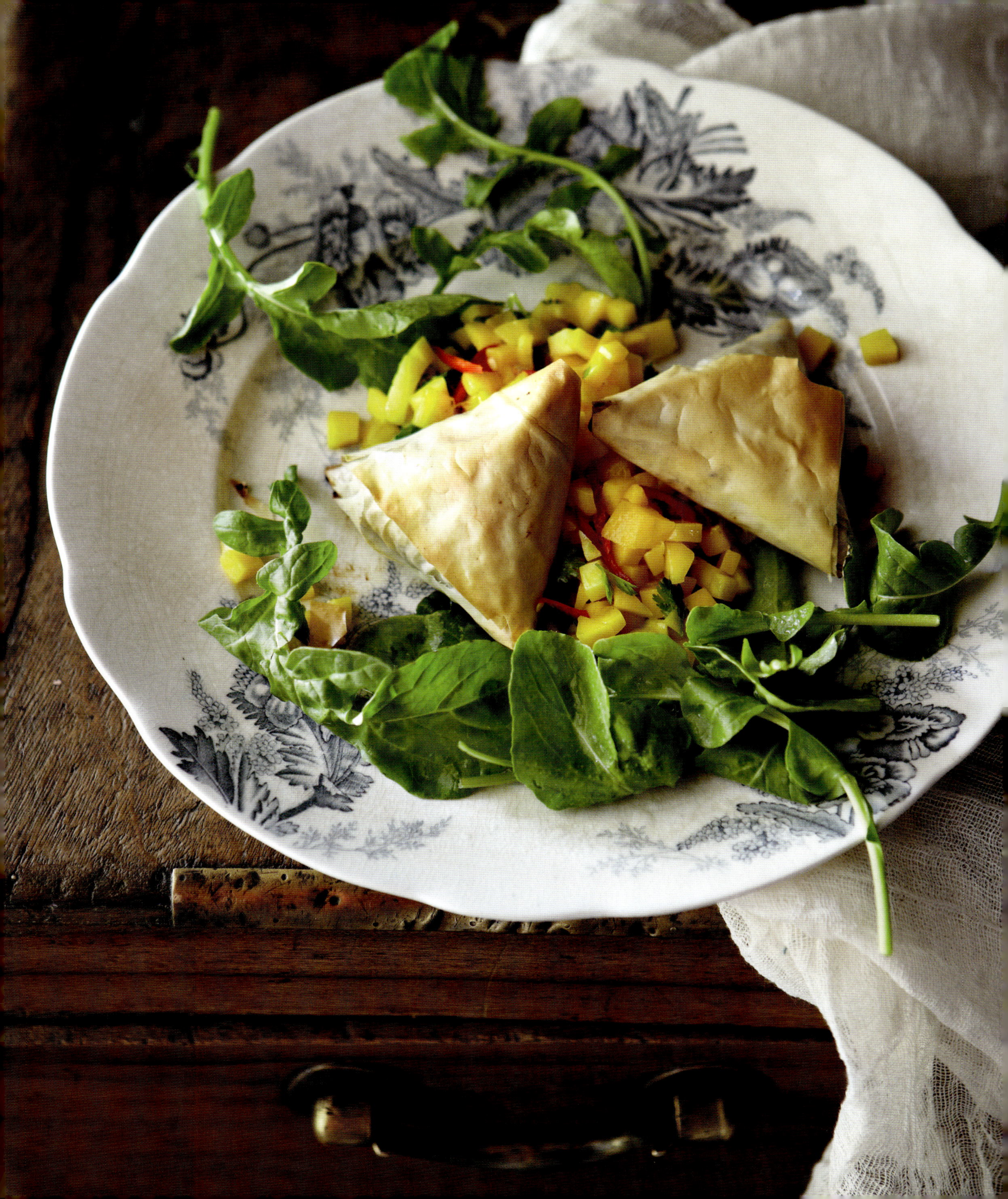

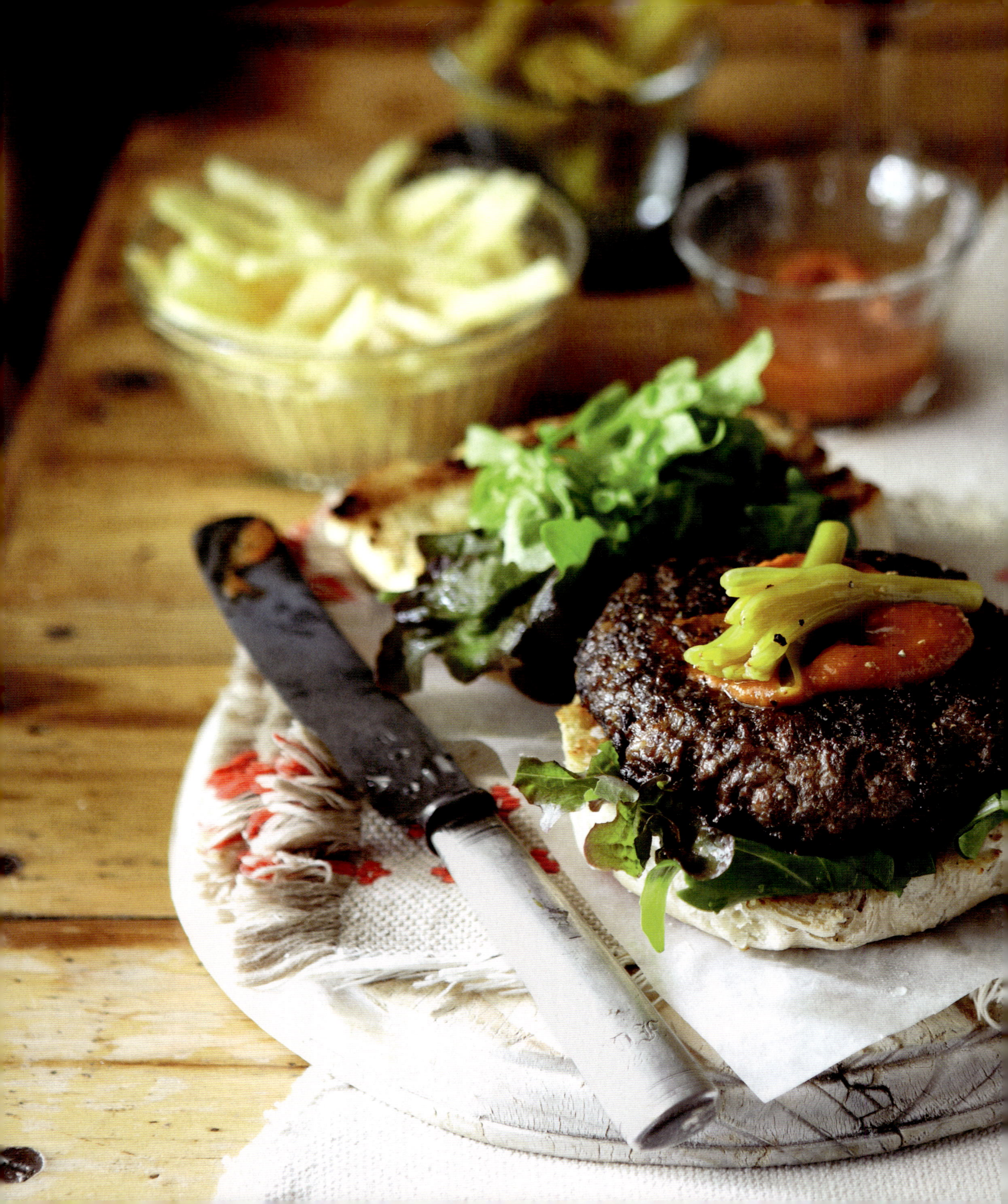

Venison burger patties

Kids love these burgers and they are a much healthier alternative to the mass-produced patties available from most supermarkets. Use only good-quality meat.

We often have these as a Saturday lunch when the 'gannets' are around. (This is what I call my boys and their neighbourhood friends, who seem to materialise every time you open the fridge. They swoop in, eat everything, leave one hell of a mess and are gone – gannets!) I make my burgers about 100 g each so 1 kg of mince should yield about 10 patties. I usually make big batches of patties and freeze them in trays so they can be easily whipped out and tossed in the pan. Try it, you'll be the toast of the neighbourhood's kids.

---

1 kg good-quality venison mince
30 ml ground coriander
30 ml ground white pepper
15 ml salt
50 g fresh rosemary, finely chopped
1 onion, finely chopped
3 cloves garlic, finely chopped
2 eggs
1 sachet (50 g) tomato paste
1 handful chopped chives

Mix all the ingredients together in a bowl and form into patties of around 100 g each (or however big you want them). Dust with a little flour so they don't stick to each other and then refrigerate for about 30 minutes so they can set.

When ready to cook, fry the patties in a little oil until they are slightly pink inside (medium to medium-well). Remember that the mince is very lean so if you overdo it they can become dry. Stack the patties on a big plate and serve with toasted buns and the family's favourite garnishings, condiments and thin chips on the side.

MAKES 10 PATTIES

Slow-cooked one-pot ostrich neck stew

What would a trip through the Karoo be without spotting some sheep, angora goats, a few springbok and, of course, the ever present, though dim-witted guardian of the veld, the humble ostrich. It may be flightless and mostly brainless, but it is a formidable beast and many an unlucky veld wanderer has been killed or severely injured by a bad-tempered male ostrich protecting its nest. It sure is tasty though and its meat is also very lean and healthy.

This is an easy one-pot meal for your slow-cooker. Just bung all the ingredients into the cooker in the morning before you head out to work and then come home to a hearty meal in the evening. Brilliant.

---

500 ml chicken stock
100 g red lentils
100 g dried sugar beans (soaking isn't necessary)
1 kg ostrich neck, cut into pieces
150 g diced bacon
4 cloves garlic, chopped
1 thumb-sized piece fresh ginger, finely chopped
1 sprig fresh rosemary
5 fresh sage leaves
3 carrots, roughly chopped
2 potatoes, peeled and quartered
4 large tomatoes, peeled and chopped
400 ml coconut milk
Salt and freshly ground pepper

Place the chicken stock, lentils and beans into the slow-cooker. Add the ostrich, bacon, garlic, ginger, herbs and vegetables. Pour in the coconut milk last and set on high for 10 minutes with the lid on. Change the setting to low and leave to cook for the whole day (or overnight) until the meat is tender and falling off the bone. Stir occasionally but be sure not to mash up the vegetables. Season to taste.

Serve over brown rice or pearled barley.

THIS RECIPE MAKES ENOUGH FOR A FAMILY OF 4

Spicy venison tripe and trotters

Whenever I hunt and am fortunate enough to take my quarry, I always try to use as much of the harvest as possible. The first four quarters are easy enough: prime cuts are used for steak, roasts and the like, while other cuts can be used to make mince, biltong and droëwors. Bones can go into stock, soups and stews. But what of the rest? The fifth quarter, so to speak.

An oft left out range of delicacies is the offal – liver, kidneys, tripe, etc. – and one of the least used bits is the tripe. Whenever I hunt I like to take the tripe. (I usually make a deal with one of the trackers or other staff where I give them half the offal, the pluck and a good tip in exchange for cleaning the tripe for me, so it's a win-win situation and we both have a nice meal or two for our families.)

This is one of my favourite methods of doing venison tripe. It's fairly easy to prepare and well worth the effort. You can vary the amount of chilli to your taste. It freezes very well so you can make a big batch and store some for a cold wintery day. Such good comfort food.

---

1 cleaned venison tripe (springbok, kudu, etc.)
Coarse salt
Freshly ground pepper
3 tomatoes, roughly chopped
2 whole chillies, seeds in
2 potatoes, roughly chopped
1 can (410 g) baked beans
500 ml good beef stock
60 ml tomato paste
10 cloves garlic
2 carrots, chopped
2 onions, roughly chopped
10 ml mustard powder
2 good handfuls chopped spinach
2 pork trotters (ask your butcher to slice them for you)

Boil the whole tripe in salted water for 2 hours, or until soft. Be sure to keep it covered with water and with the lid on for the duration. Once cooked, drain, rinse and allow to cool.

While the tripe is cooling, prep your veg. When the tripe is cool enough to handle, chop it into bite-sized pieces and place in a large slow-cooker or casserole dish. Add seasoning and the rest of the ingredients and simmer gently with the lid on for a further 3 hours, or until the meat is falling off the bone and the beans have cooked away into a thick sauce.

Serve with peppery mash and a glass of Pinot Noir.

SERVES 6–8

Venison, Parma ham and mushroom lasagne

This is a rather extravagant lasagne recipe that I came across whilst on a slow food tour of Italy. The HQ of the Slow Food movement in Bra, Piedmont, has its own restaurant called Osteria del Boccondivino (Place of the divine mouthful). I had a most memorable lunch there and was so taken by a similar dish (veal mince, mushroom and Parma lasagne) that I went into the kitchen and chatted to the chef (in my very best Italian) and got the basic recipe from him. This is my own Karoo adaptation of it using springbok mince and my homemade (F)arma ham and pasta. Feel free to experiment with your own version of this recipe and let me know how it turns out. Have fun!

---

45 ml butter
1 onion, finely chopped
300 g mushrooms, roughly chopped
60 ml cake flour
1 litre milk
60 ml grated Parmesan cheese
10 ml grated nutmeg
500 g springbok mince (or any good-quality venison or beef mince)
4 cloves garlic, chopped
Chopped fresh rosemary
Salt and freshly ground pepper
16 sheets good-quality lasagne
300 g baby spinach or morogo (wild African spinach)
Finely sliced Parma ham
45 g cubed butter
250 g mozzarella cheese, grated (optional)

Preheat the oven to 180 °C. Grease a large ovenproof dish.

Melt the butter in a large saucepan and sweat the onion until soft. Add the mushrooms, cover the saucepan and simmer for 20 minutes. Gradually add the flour, and then the milk just as slowly. Stir non-stop and cook for another 5 minutes. Stir in half the Parmesan and all the nutmeg, then remove from the heat and set aside.

In a separate pan, fry the mince with the chopped garlic and rosemary until cooked. Add salt and pepper to taste.

Cook the lasagne sheets for 1 minute in boiling water (if you're not using fresh lasagne).

Place alternate layers of lasagne, mince, mushroom mixture, spinach and Parma ham in the prepared dish until the dish is full. Dot with the cubes of butter and the rest of the Parmesan (and grated mozzarella, if using).

Bake for 20 minutes and serve with a herb salad and a good Sangiovese.

SERVES 4–6

'Slow food unites the pleasure of food with responsibility, sustainability and harmony with nature.'
Carlo Petrini, Slow Food® founder and president (www.slowfood.com)

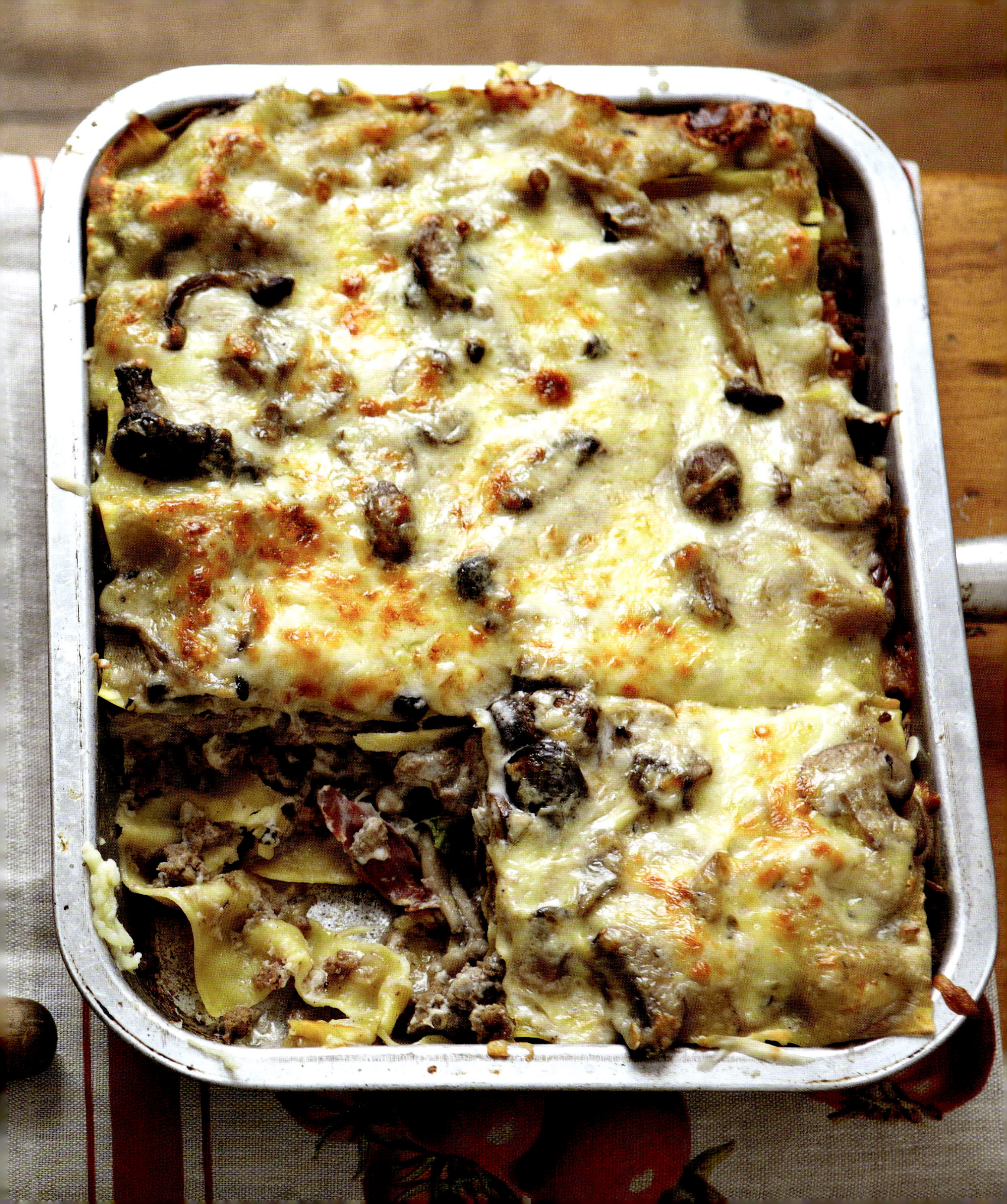

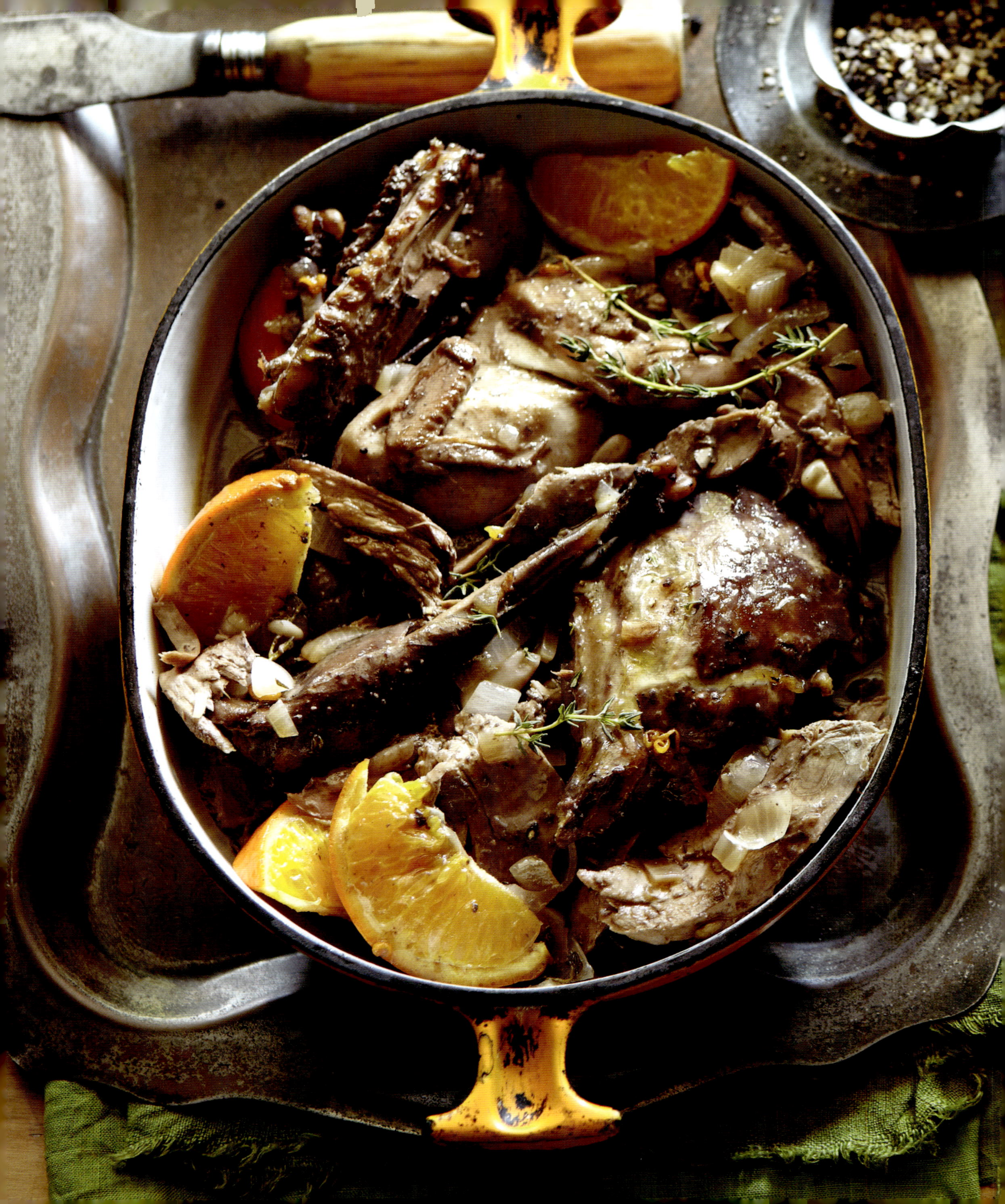

Game bird potjie with oranges and ginger

Wingshooting is one of my all-time favourite pastimes, apart from fly-fishing, hunting, cooking, driving nice cars, drinking good wine and puffing on the occasional cigar.

My mate Tim van Heerden owns and runs the company Karoo Wingshooting. During season he is out in the mountains with clients looking for grey-winged partridge, pigeons, guinea fowl and all sorts of wonderful game birds. Naturally, I love to get out and stretch my legs in the Karoo mountains and whenever Tim invites me along, I am more than game (if you'll excuse the pun). He has a good pair of pointers and birding in the Karoo mountains over a good set of dogs is one of the true pleasures in life. Real bucket list stuff.

Two of my favourite things to hunt over dogs are guinea fowl and grey-winged partridge. Guinea fowl are wily, deceptive and move incredibly fast through the undergrowth. Grey-winged partridge on the other hand is even more difficult and is considered one of the toughest game birds to hunt. Its habitat is typically at over 1 500 m above sea level, where the terrain is rugged and the air is thin. Grey-winged hunting is not for the faint of heart, nor the unfit. Hunting them over a brace of pointers is very difficult but also very addictive; you can walk 10–15 km in a day in very rough terrain and they will sit tight until the very last second, when they explode in a cacophony of feathers and noise from virtually under your feet. It is a real challenge and you will certainly earn every bird you get.

This recipe pays homage to the two champion game birds that, in my humble opinion, are the best. It's good for a small crowd and will be an absolute winner with your friends.

Knob of unsalted butter
3 red onions, roughly chopped
8 cloves garlic, finely chopped
2 thumb-sized pieces fresh ginger, finely chopped
2 grey-winged partridges, cleaned and portioned
1 guinea fowl, cleaned and portioned
Salt and freshly ground pepper
4 oranges, halved
Zest from 1 orange
500 ml chicken stock
1 handful fresh thyme
4 large carrots, cut into big chunks
1 handful broccoli florets (or any crisp seasonal veg)

Melt the butter in a hot no. 3 (or bigger) potjie and sweat off the onions, garlic and ginger. Add the bird portions and brown, salting and peppering as necessary. Once browned, squeeze the juice of 3 of the oranges into the pot. Add the zest, chicken stock, thyme and carrots, and give it all a good stir. Place the remaining orange halves on top (flesh side down), close the lid and reduce the heat so that the pot never reaches more than a gentle simmer.

Remember the golden rules with a potjie: once the lid is on, never lift it or stir the pot unless someone's life depends on it; and a pot that boils, is a pot that spoils.

Allow the pot to bubble very gently (not boil) for about 3 hours. You want to see one constant but faint little steam funnel escaping from the pot and hear a very gentle bubbling when you put your ear to the pot. That is all!

Add the broccoli to the pot about 15 minutes before serving, and remove the orange halves, squeezing out the remaining juice as you do so. (Don't be tempted to stir though!)

Once ready, remove the pot from the heat and get ready to rumble. Serve over pearled wheat with a magnificent Chardonnay or even a robust Chenin Blanc

SERVES 5–8

Charcuterie and Deli Cuts

During the Second World War a number of Italian prisoners of war (POWs) were sent to work on Karoo farms as labourers. Apart from being POWs, they were also artisans of all kinds before the war and thus utilised these skills whilst here. A number of well-designed buildings, roads and bridges in the area still testify to this. They also left a culinary legacy that can be seen in the style of salamis, sausages and cured meats of this region, particularly in the use of venison (as a substitute for the more traditional pork), which was the one meat source still in abundance and relatively freely available in the Karoo during those ration years.

Now I have no Italian blood in me to speak of but my fascination with the natural curing and preserving of meats was really piqued during my first trip to Italy, as I noticed such glaring similarities in methodology, ingredients and climate. I needed to know more and a passion was born.

I had been experimenting with charcuterie for a while before I made the trip, but all the techniques I had found were very modern and complicated and full of artificial preservatives, additives and the like. I was starting to become disillusioned with the process, but this changed when I went over to see for myself how it was done in the classical, time-honoured manner. During the trip I had the privilege of meeting a ninth-generation butcher, and what an experience it was. This guy had such an instinctive knowledge of meat that it was ingrained in his blood. His family has owned their small butchery, in the same building, for nearly 900 years. He was heading towards retirement and about to hand over to his son, the tenth generation!

I learnt many, many things while in Italy, but the most important lessons I gleaned were that simplicity, superb base ingredients, spectacularly good cuts of meat, time and patience were the keys I was missing.

When I got home, I was so inspired and motivated to make hams and salamis in this old-fashioned way that I immediately started searching out the finest pork, venison and other meats. After much more trial and error, I was pleasantly surprised with the end result. Gary Player's old adage of 'the harder I practice, the luckier I get' rang true.

Of course, there were some disappointments along the way, but knowledge gained through experience is usually attained through the lessons of failure and then success.

The fundamental basic ingredients to traditional charcuterie are very simple: salt, garlic, fresh rosemary, very good-quality meat, time and patience. There is no quick-fix.

This same ethos must be applied to smoking, pickling, curing and drying of all sorts of meats. I am constantly experimenting with ways to do all these things. Bacon by one's own hand is unbelievable, even if it is just me who thinks so.

One of my finer inventions is lightly smoked trout using honeybush tea. As smoking is one of the key aspects of charcuterie, I built my own primitive smoker. A retired steel filing cabinet now sports a chimney, and the shelves are no longer used for files and books but have been replaced by racks that now file heaps of sausages, cheese, venison, pork and fish. It works beautifully.

My biggest triumph, however, is that I have finally managed to create my own version of the legendary Parma ham or prosciutto. I call it 'Farma' ham and though it takes over a year to make from start to finish, I am very proud of it. If you have the time and inclination to try it, the recipe is on the following pages, as are a whole range of different and delicious bits of charcuterie and other tasty 'deli' cuts I have managed to perfect over the years. Remember, charcuterie is a bit of a dark art but with practice, perseverance and patience the results are unbelievably rewarding and tasty.

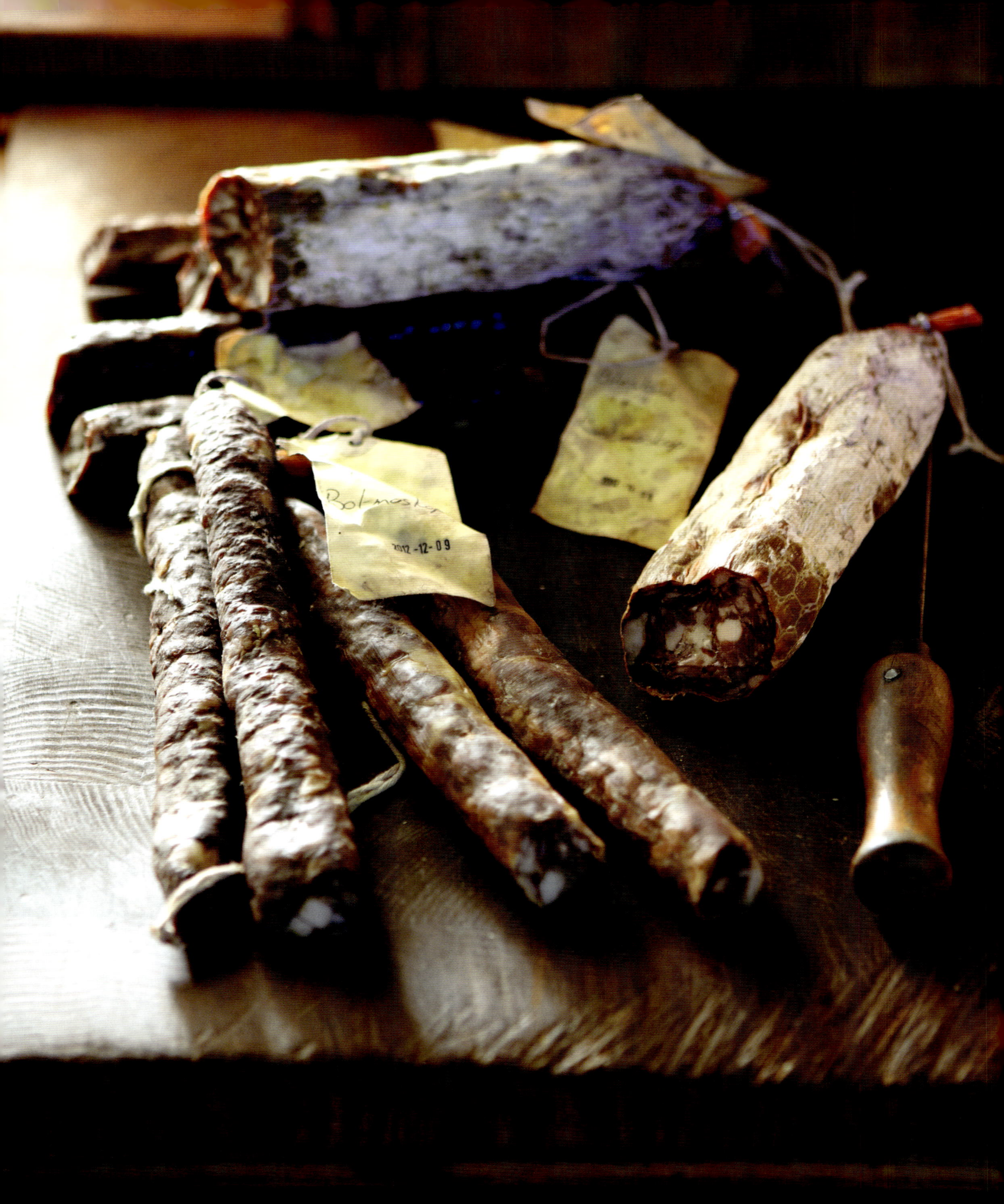
2012-12-09

Venison salami

Good salami is one of life's simple pleasures that I just can't seem to get enough of. Traditionally made with pork, I have been experimenting with different types of salami for a few years now, with mixed results. Venison, however, makes wonderful salami and here is a basic recipe that should be good for about three full-sized salamis. You need to be patient and check them daily, but they are wonderful when they are ready.

Remember that salami-making should only be attempted during the cold winter months and that it is not an exact science. Only patience and perseverance will ensure a good result. Also make notes as you go along so you can see at what stage different things happen, or if you make a mistake you can retrace your steps. Of course, when it does work out, you will also have an accurate record for the next batch.

Have fun though and remember to think of me when you have that first perfect slice of your own authentic salami.

3.5 kg venison (preferably shoulder or leg roast cuts), cut into 5 cm cubes
1 kg fatty pork, cut into 5 cm cubes
1.5 g saltpetre (be very specific with this amount, no more)
150 g coarse salt
150 g cracked coloured peppercorns
100 g mustard seeds (mixed yellow and black whole seed)
200 g paprika
20 cloves garlic, finely chopped
250 ml finely chopped fresh rosemary
375 ml good red wine
500 g pork fat or spek, cut into 1 cm cubes and chilled
250 g brown sugar
Salami or hog casings (ask your supplier or butcher)

Mix the venison and fatty pork together with the saltpetre, spices, garlic and rosemary. Mince through a coarse (8 mm) mincing plate. Add the wine and the chilled fat and mix well using your hands. Refrigerate overnight.

Stuff the mixture tightly into salami or hog casings and tie off the ends. Prick the casings all over with a pin to allow air to penetrate. Weigh each salami and make a note thereof. Hang for 1 day at a temperature of 20–30 °C to allow the fermentation process to start. After this, hang at a temperature of between 13 and 15 °C and a humidity of 70%.

Hang for about 2 weeks, with a good draught, checking daily for strange smells and too much shrinkage. A bit of white mould, similar to cheese mould, is good (green, blue or grey is bad). The salamis should be ready when they have lost 25–30% of their weight (this is where the original weights come in handy) yet are still firm and fairly pliable to the touch. Keep sealed and refrigerated until you want to use them.

MAKES 3 FULL-SIZED SALAMIS

Simple venison sausage

A tasty venison sausage is one of the finest things in life. Either in the pan, grilled or, best of all, on the braai. Man, I get all teary eyed just thinking about it.

It is also so simple to make. This basic wors *(sausage) recipe can be used for just about any venison, so don't worry that I am using kudu, it's what I had in hand at the time. I often like to mix a few different types of meat together, which is really delicious. A few basic principles must be applied though, so stick to these and you will have great sausage every time. Don't, and you will have cr*p sausage every time.*

---

7 kg kudu meat, cut into 5 cm cubes
2 kg fatty pork meat, cubed
1 kg mutton fat, cubed
200 g coarse salt
100 g cracked black pepper
100 g fresh rosemary, finely chopped
50 g whole mustard seeds
50 g cracked coriander seeds
1 litre iced water
No. 24–26 sheep sausage casings

Mix all the meat together.* Mix all the spices together and add to the meat mix. Mix well by hand and allow to stand overnight in the fridge.

When ready to fill the sausage casings, mince using the coarse mincing plate (8 mm) and then pour over 1 litre filtered iced water (see golden rules). Don't mix the mince again.

Fill the sausage casings and hang overnight in a cool place, ideally a cold room or fridge (most of the water will drip out at this stage so be sure to have something underneath to catch this 'juice').

MAKES ABOUT 10 KG

* If you want to make *droëwors* (dried sausage), omit the pork and add extra mutton or venison to the mix. Hang the wet sausage in a cool, dry, well-ventilated place for a few days until it's ready.

Golden rules for sausage-making

- Use only the best meat you can get – a lot of people think sausage is made with all the leftover bits. This is true only of bad sausage. Good meat = good sausage.
- When it comes to spices, less is more. Rather add a bit of salt after the fact. If it is too salty or too spicy, you can't undo that. Always cook and taste a little of your spiced mince before you fill the casings. That way you can adjust the spice mix if you need to. It's too late to try to fix after the sausage has been filled.
- Once the meat has been minced, try not to mix it again. The less you mess with the mince the better. Fill the sausage and be done with it.
- Pour 1 litre of quality, filtered iced water over the spiced mince just before you fill the casings, it helps to lubricate the casings and eases the filling process.
- Let your newly filled sausages hang overnight. This allows the flavours to develop and the excess fluid to drip out.
- Don't be tempted to put anything but quality meat and spices into your sausage. Many people will tell you to add all sorts of ingredients like breadcrumbs, soya, etc. – don't do it. If you want commercially manufactured sausage with all the junk in it, go buy it from a shady butcher rather than spend all that time and effort making rubbish for yourself.
- The rules for making good sausage are the same as the rules of life: what you put in is what you get out …

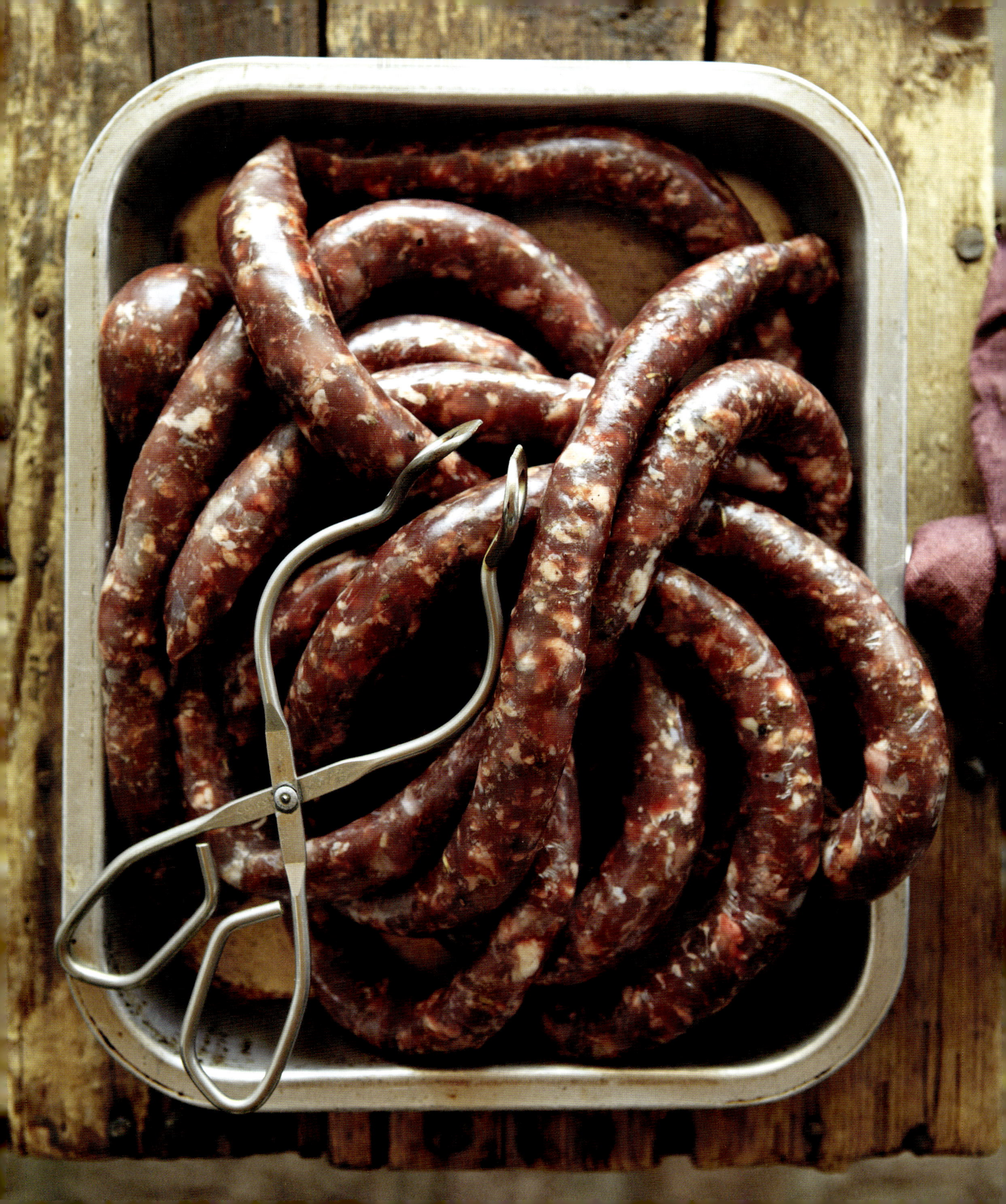

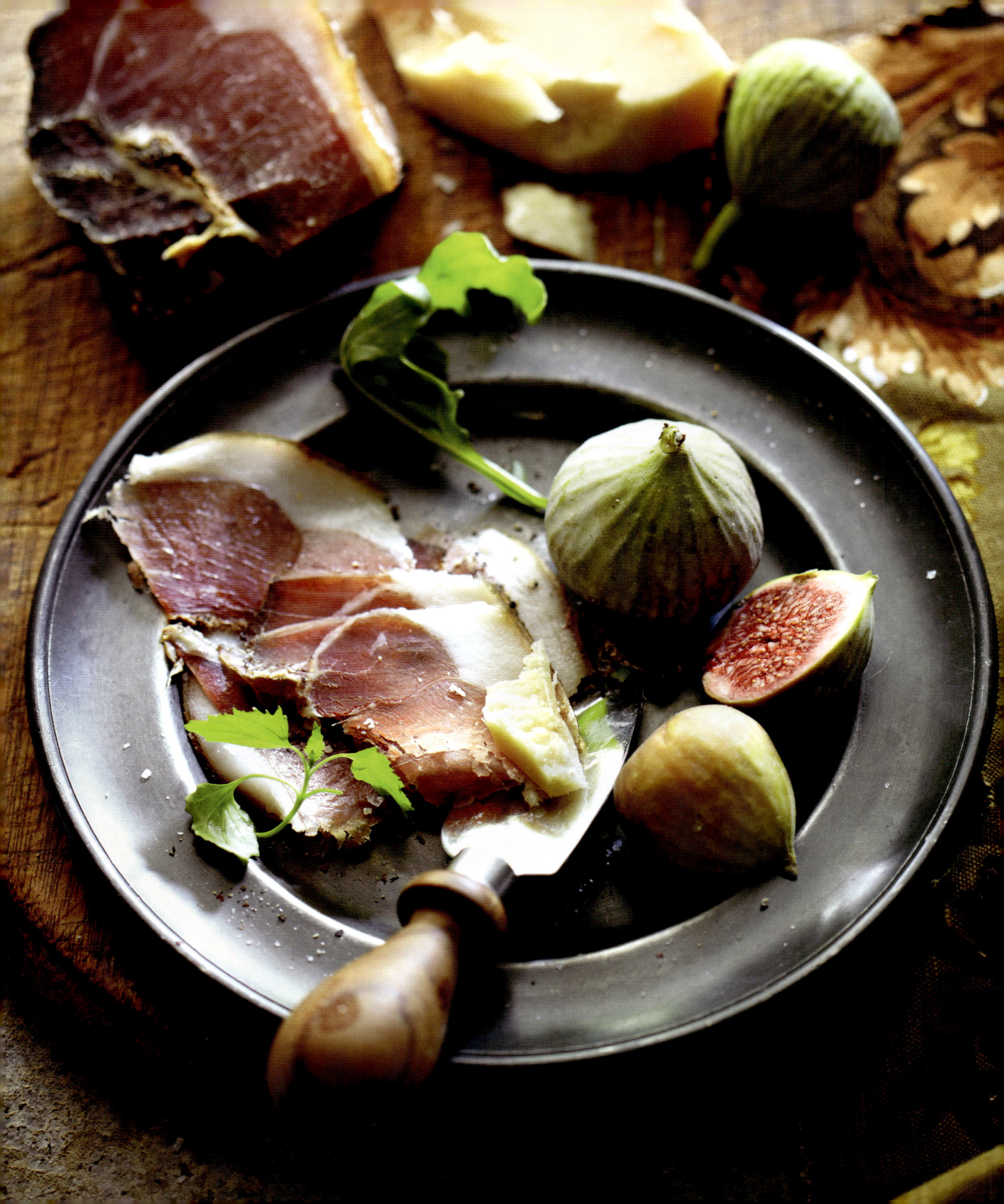

My own 'Farma' ham (Prosciutto di Karoo)

What would the world be without friends? My great mate Graham Harris, his lovely wife Helen and their four daughters, farm fabulous Karoo lamb and angora goats on their farm Taaintjiesview in the Kendrew district, about 25 km from Graaff-Reinet. For the home kitchen, Graham keeps a few pigs. With a little goading from me he has them running free-range and eating only the best food a pig could want. As he farms his pigs exactly the way I need them to be farmed – wholesome and good – I get my pork only from him. I take them vegetable trimmings from our restaurant gardens too and the porkers really love these.

In the old days when we were still living in the city, we seldom had the opportunity to acquire a whole pig for ourselves, so I had some learning and experimenting to do here. I like to get my pork in at a certain weight, with a nice layer of fat under the skin, clean and pure white. The Italians use a lot of pork and I learnt so much while I was there. I spent time at a school of charcuterie, the Istituto Lattiero-Caseario di Moretta e delle Tecnologie Agroalimentari, in the small town of Moretta in the Piemonte region, where Emilia Brezzo teaches. She taught me so much about the art of artisanal charcuterie. Together with her husband Lodoviko and their three children, they have become close family friends.

The most important lesson I learnt when making real prosciutto is that you need three key ingredients to make a great ham: really good-quality pigs, very good-quality salt, and lots of patience.

Pork fat is one of the purest forms of fat and is very easily assimilated into the human body; it is also very healthy. The problem comes in when pigs are fed all sorts of rubbish, including growth hormones. All the excess and toxins are stored in the fat, as with most animals, but more so with pork, and this manifests in the flavour, fat and meat of the animal. The upside of this is that the converse is also true, so if you give your piggies only the best food and greens, then the meat, fat and flavour will be absolutely supreme.

Through trial and error I managed to get these hams just right, but not before I lost a lot of good hog legs and nearly my sanity. This method of making hams should only be attempted in the winter months. Don't be despondent if you don't get it right first (or second, or third) time. Perseverance, patience and attention to detail will get you there.

---

1 whole free-range, organic hog leg (about 15 kg)
1 kg good-quality coarse sea salt (maybe more)
40 g ground black pepper
20 g ground juniper berries
140 g garlic, roughly chopped
60 g fresh rosemary, chopped
60 g mustard seeds, crushed

LARD MIXTURE
1 kg lard
200 g ground white pepper

First and crucially, you need to massage the outside of the leg (the skin) to get all the blood out of the visible blood vessels. This is hard, laborious work but essential. Next, rub the salt and all the herbs and spices into the leg. Leave a generous covering over the exposed meat (i.e. not the skin).

Refrigerate, uncovered, for 2 weeks. After 2 weeks, repeat the process, and pack more salty spice on the exposed meat. Refrigerate for a further 2 weeks.

Rinse off the excess cure and hang the leg for 50 days at 15 °C and 70% humidity. After this period, trim off all the dried bits and edges and cover the exposed meat with a mixture of lard and white pepper.

Hang for 12 months, checking daily for any green or yellow mould or bad smells. If you detect any of these bad moulds, wipe them off with some fresh lemon juice. (If this does not work and it starts to rot, then I am afraid you will have to toss the whole leg and start again. Eish!) Once again, white mould is fine. Good luck!

MAKES 1 HAM

Kirsten Short's cured venison sirloin

Wheatlands Sport Club is about 55 km south of Graaff-Reinet and has a long and rich history. It was founded in the early 1880s, at the same time as the Harefield Cricket Club moved in. The cricketers kept their name and in 2011 they celebrated their 130th anniversary. The club also boasts a bowling green, tennis courts and a very large 'swimming pool' (it's actually a swimming dam, but brilliant for a dip after a long afternoon on the cricket field).

As is the nature of country cricket, I have turned out for Harefield on occasion – usually when they are superbly desperate for players and are really scraping the bottom of the barrel. Otherwise we tend to meet regularly in league fixtures when playing for my regular team, Bethesda Road CC. It's always a social affair with loads of banter, good humour and the occasional bit of cricket in between.

Dave and Kirsten Short are the family's eighth generation at Wheatlands and, together with brother Lloyd and wife Janine (who farm next door), they have taken over the reins from their mom and dad, Arthur and Di. They are pretty much the backbone and driving force behind the sports club today.

Due to the nature of such things, the clubhouse and facilities are in constant need of attention, maintenance and upgrade and there are regular fundraising events held at the club throughout the year. They are always wonderful occasions with what seems like the whole community in attendance. At one such event I got a wonderful recipe from Kirsten for a cured carpaccio-style sirloin which I absolutely loved. And now I share it with you.

---

1 whole springbok sirloin (you can use any venison sirloin; I prefer springbok)
125 ml brown sugar
125 ml coarse salt
125 ml cracked black pepper
1 good handful chopped fresh thyme
1 good handful chopped fresh rosemary

Mix all the ingredients together and rub onto the meat, leaving in place a generous coating. Make sure that every part of the sirloin is covered. Wrap the coated sirloin in plastic wrap and refrigerate for 3 days to cure and to allow the flavours to infuse.

After 3 days, unwrap and dust off most of the curing mixture. Rewrap and freeze until ready to use.

When you want to serve the sirloin, remove it from the freezer and unwrap. Cut very thin slices from the frozen meat – as much as you need. If you keep it frozen it is easier to slice and the unused portion can just be wrapped again and popped back into the freezer for future use (for up to 3 months).

Serve with cheese and biscuits and an onion marmalade.

SERVES ABOUT 20

Spicy hunter's salami

I like to make this thin little salami and take it into the veld when I am hunting; it's very tasty and makes a great snack. If you don't want the zing, just leave out the chilli. Otherwise it's a great variation on the traditional salami. Once again, only make these during the cool winter months.

4.5 kg venison, cut into 5 cm cubes
3 kg lean pork meat, cut into 5 cm cubes
280 g coarse salt
150 g hot chillies, seeded and chopped
500 ml red wine
1 large handful cracked black pepper
1 large handful mustard seeds
500 g brown sugar
500 g pork fat, cut into 2.5 cm cubes
No. 28–32 hog casings

Mix all the salami ingredients, except the pork fat, together until combined. Mince through a coarse (8 mm) mincing plate. Add the pork fat and mix well.

Using a sausage stuffer, fill the casings, tying them off at about 30 cm intervals. Tie up the salamis and hang them in loops in a well-ventilated, 20–30 °C, dry spot (they must not touch each other) for 1 day to ripen.

On the second day, in the evening (for this stage you need a cooler temp of 13–18 °C), lay the salamis on a table and cover them with a plank and some weights. In the morning, hang them up again until the evening, and then repeat what you did the evening before. Do this for a further 5–6 days.

Hang for a further 2 days. They should be ready when they have lost about 35% of their weight but are still fairly moist inside.

I like to store them in a fridge when they are ready. They will keep drying out the longer they stay there so be sure to enjoy them before that.

MAKES ABOUT 5 KG OF FINISHED SALAMI

Homemade smoked bacon

Homemade bacon is one of those rare treats that is actually really easy to make if you have some time and a smoker. This method works very well and can be used to make kassler chops, eisbein, hams and the like. For this recipe I use pork belly, but you can use other cuts, just ask your butcher to advise you. You will also need to pickle for a bit longer if you are pickling with the bone in.

2 whole pork bellies, each cut into a rectangular shape (about 1.5 kg each)

FOR THE BRINE
5 litres salt water solution (mix as much coarse salt as you can into warm water until the salt will no longer dissolve and a whole raw egg floats in it)
1 handful black peppercorns
150 g brown sugar
4 bay leaves
60 g mustard seeds
5 cloves garlic, unpeeled and bruised
2 sprigs fresh rosemary
1 lemon, quartered

Mix all the brine ingredients in a large plastic or stainless steel container, cool completely and then drop in the pork. Set aside in a cool place (the fridge is ideal) for 3 days, ensuring the bellies are completely submerged for the duration.

After 3 days remove the pork from the brine and soak for 2 hours in tepid water. Pat dry and allow to rest in the fridge overnight.

When ready to smoke the bacon, ensure it is completely dry and at room temperature. Smoke over a cold smoke for 3–4 hours, or until the bacon is golden brown in colour. Once you take it out of the smoker, leave it to settle overnight and then you are good to go.

Cut yourself a nice thick slice, slap it in the pan and have a good old-fashioned fry up.

If wrapped in plastic wrap and frozen, it should keep for up to 6 months, if you can resist it for that long.

MAKES ABOUT 3 KG

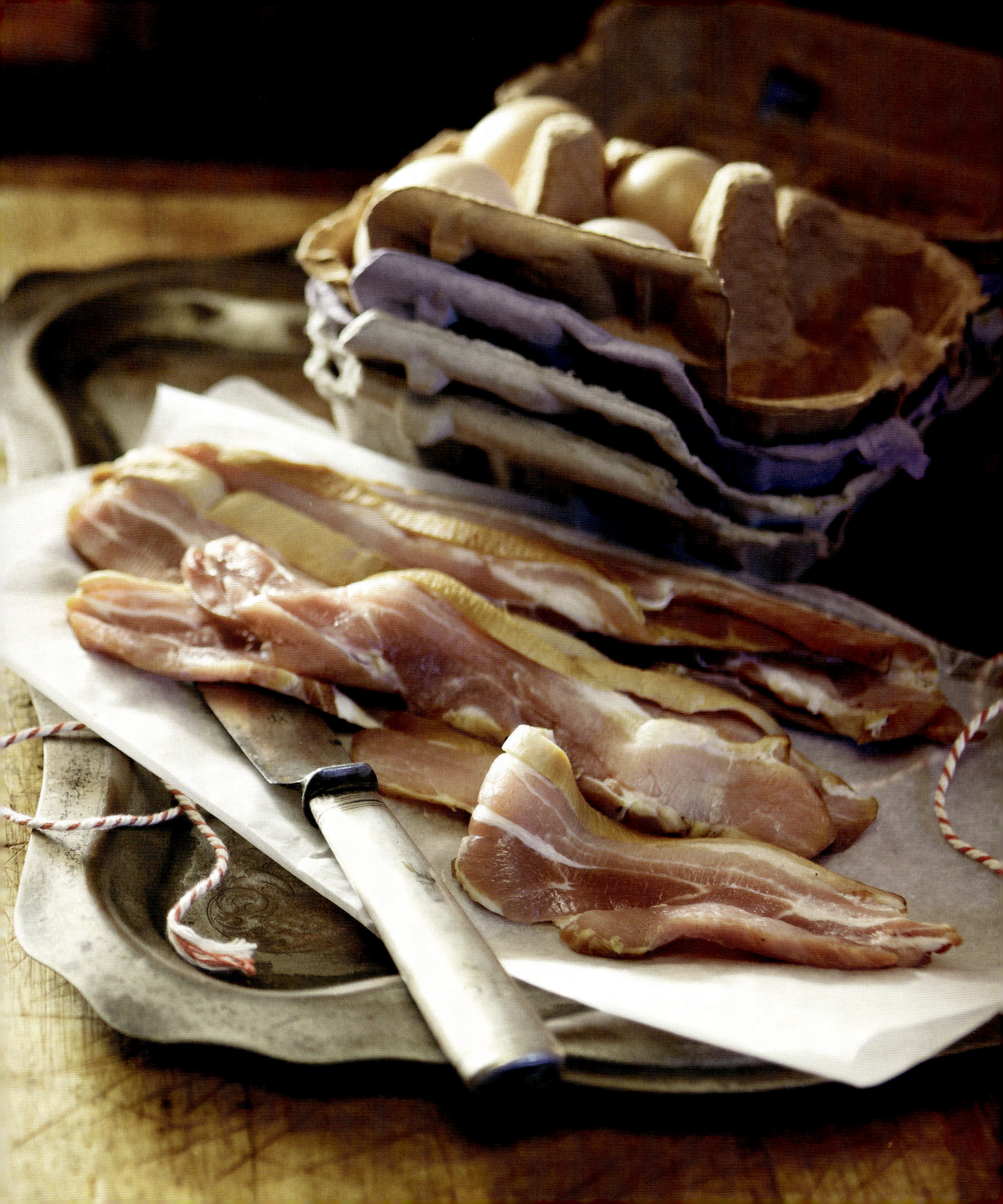

Fennel and lamb sausages

So you think you should only use lamb for roasts, chops and stews? Well here is a variation for the braai or pan. It's nice and herby and full of delicate flavour.

1 kg lamb (rump, shoulder or neck)
100 g lamb fat
2 cloves garlic, chopped
100 g potatoes, peeled and boiled
½ stalk fennel, chopped
750 ml milk
2–3 eggs
2 handfuls fresh herbs (rosemary, thyme and flat-leaf parsley)
50 g fennel seeds
10 ml coriander seeds
Freshly ground pepper
Lamb casings or meat gauze

Cut the lamb and fat into smaller pieces and grind it with a meat grinder.

Mix the garlic, boiled potatoes and fennel together and run them through the grinder.

Mix all the ground ingredients with the milk and eggs. Chop the herbs and stir them into the ground meat with all the spices. Fry a small piece of the mixture to ensure that it is seasoned correctly. Adjust seasoning, if necessary.

Stuff the casings or roll the mixture into a meat net or gauze. Chill the sausages for 30–60 minutes before frying or grilling.

MAKES 12–14 SAUSAGES

Cheesy warthog and herb sausage

Twin brothers Angus and Will Pringle are hunting buddies of mine. Though Angus lives in East London (he's a hot-shot attorney there), his twin brother William recently moved to Graaff-Reinet as the headmaster of Union High School. Angus was a client of mine when I was still in the banking world, but we soon realised that we had a common love for the outdoors and hunting, which was a magnificent distraction from the rigours of the corporate hamster wheel. This commonality ensured that our friendship grew and we make a point of hunting together a few times a year. One of our favourite hunts is warthog. Angus has a butcher friend who makes the best warthog cheese sausages I have ever tasted, so I decided to come up with my own version. I added a bit of fresh fennel seed to the recipe as fennel works so well with pork and is not easily overpowered by the cheese.

5 kg warthog meat, cut into 5 cm cubes
50 g thyme
50 g oregano
100 g fennel seeds
150 g coarse salt
100 g cracked black pepper
1 kg Cheddar cheese, grated
1 litre iced water
No. 24–26 sheep sausage casings

Mix the meat with the herbs and spices until well combined. Mince through a coarse (8 mm) mincing plate.

Once minced, sprinkle the cheese and water over the meat and mix lightly. Fill the casings immediately and then hang overnight to allow the flavours to develop. You can cold smoke this sausage too if you're looking for an extra-rich flavour.

MAKES 5 KG

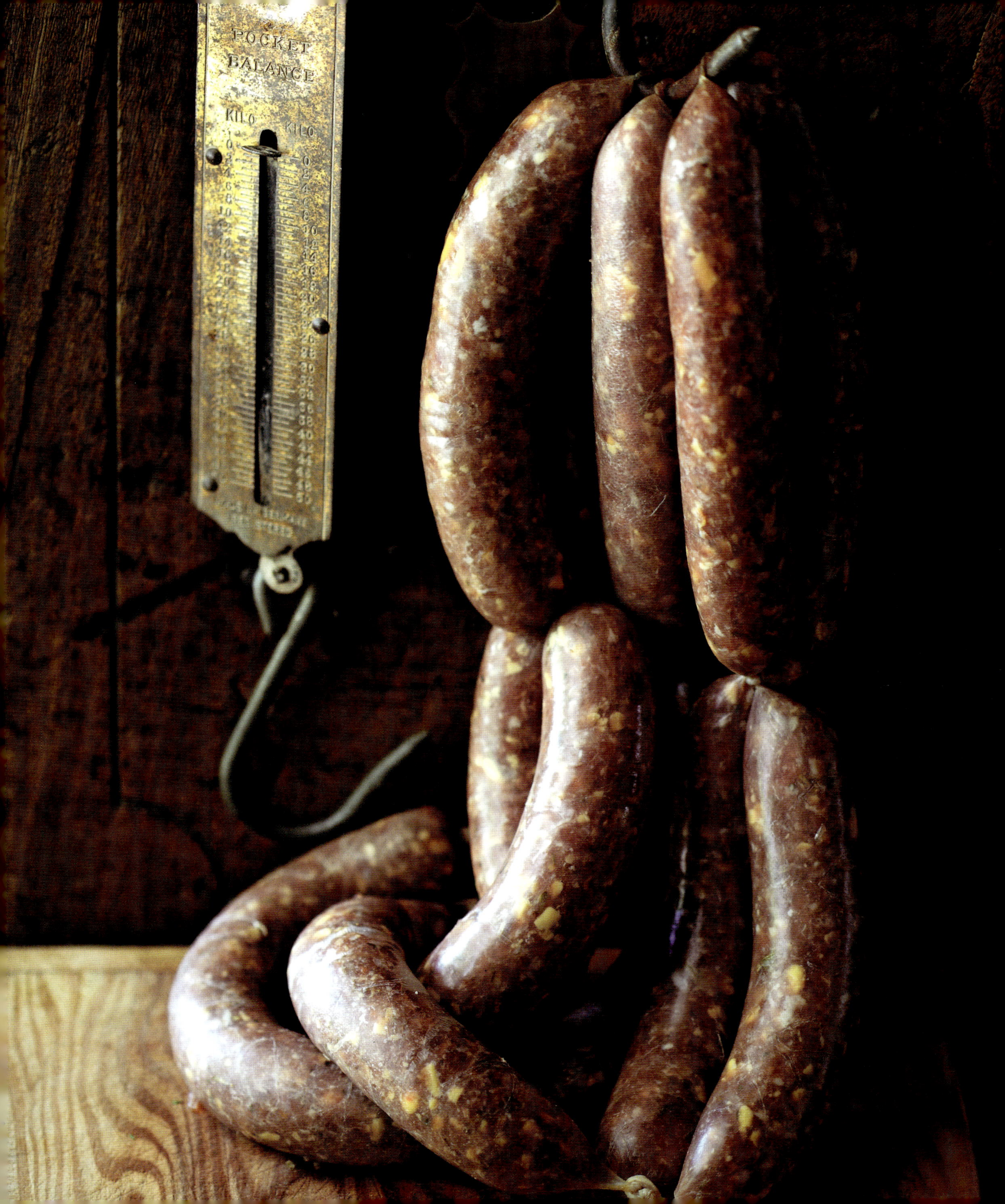
POCKET
BALANCE
KILO
KILO

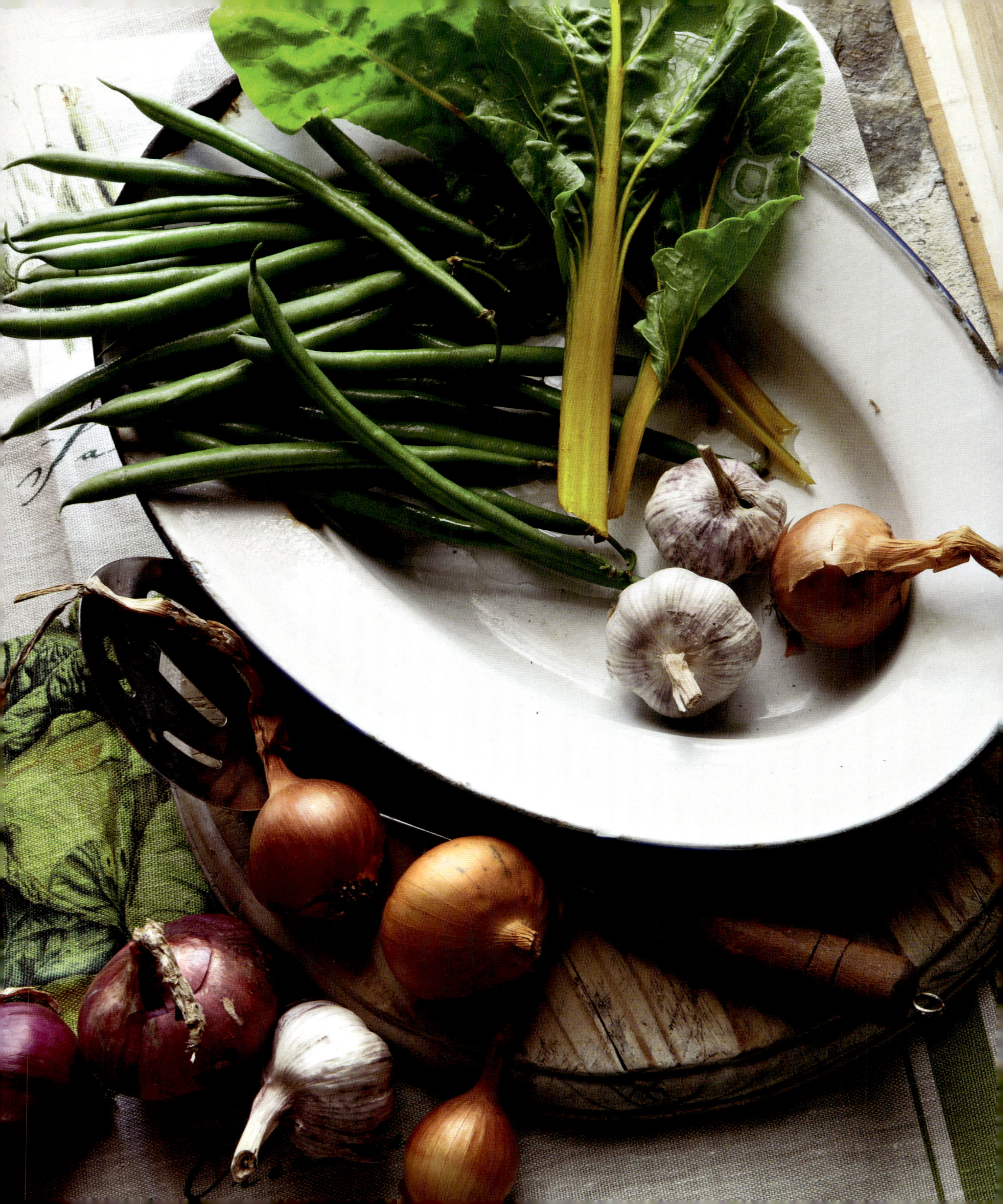

Sides and vegetables

I love my veggie garden. I'm not a great or very talented gardener and I think that is why I get such immense satisfaction when I manage to grow a good crop of fresh, tasty and healthy vegetables. Homegrown veg, no matter what it is, tastes better. That's a fact.

My right-hand man George is gardener-in-chief and he has such a feel for the earth and what's going on in the garden that we have a plethora of fresh vegetables for the restaurant and home on a daily basis.

We have a very cool and fairly good system. I plan the menus according to the season and chat to our manager Charlotte, who then plans the planting and co-ordinates with George to make it happen. I end up running around loading up manure (lucky me) from various farms, making sure that all kitchen scraps and trimmings go into the compost heap and George, Charlotte and the gardening team ensure I have fresh organic veg available for dinner every evening. Quite often we have too much of everything, which is great too as the staff get to take home any excess.

I believe it's possible for almost everyone to have access to fresh homegrown vegetables. All it takes is a little effort and initiative. A family of four could easily supply a large portion of their daily veg using a space no bigger than a front door.

As a Slow Food ambassador, I am very keen on a project they run called '1 000 Gardens in Africa'. It's not just any garden though; it is the result of the development of many agricultural and educational projects already underway. Vegetable plots are farmed sustainably, using composting techniques, natural treatments for pests, rational water use, local plant varieties and by intercropping fruit trees, vegetables and medicinal herbs. The basic premise is to allow the people of Africa to feed themselves, healthily, cheaply and sustainably. I would add another '-ly' here and include 'tastily'.

I try to use only heritage seed as you can always keep some seed back and replant, meaning your vegetables get cheaper and cheaper. I have even started a seed bank and swop seeds with my friends and guests all the time. It's a great way to keep new and interesting vegetables growing in your garden.

To get you excited and to prove that I'm not just a meat-freak, I've got fabulous veggie recipes in this chapter. So get into the garden or get one started, even in pots if there's no space, and eat more homegrown veg.

Rose's decadent savoury and sweet Christmas tart

Rose made this one Christmas a few years ago when she was expecting some friends for a morning tea. It was such a hit that everyone wanted the recipe.

The base is essentially a white sauce, so that's where you start, and then you add all the other tasty bits, mix in the eggs (which help it set) and pop it in the oven to bake. It has such a crazy range of flavours and textures you are sure to be the hit of the tea party.

Flour, for dusting
Melted butter
Olive oil
1–2 large onions, chopped
Pinch of dried Italian herbs
100 g streaky bacon, chopped
100 g lardons (thickly cut cubes of bacon)
1 clove garlic, chopped
50 g almonds
150 g mixed nuts
50 g butter
50 g cake flour
250 ml milk
Salt and lemon pepper
4 eggs, lightly beaten
Green fig preserve (about 5 figs, quartered)
1 wedge of apricot or similar blue cheese

Preheat the oven to 180 °C. Sprinkle flour over the base of an ovenproof tart dish and pour in a little melted butter, just enough to leave a thin film on the base.

Heat a little olive oil in a pan and lightly fry the onions and Italian herbs. Remove from the pan and set aside.

Using the same pan, fry the streaky bacon until crisp. Remove from the pan and set aside. Fry the lardons in the same pan until crisp and then remove from the pan and set aside. Fry the garlic lightly and remove the pan from the heat.

Dry-roast the almonds and mixed nuts in a clean pan. Chop and roast again lightly. Set aside.

Melt the butter and gradually stir in the flour. Cook over low heat for 1 minute. Gradually add the milk, stirring continuously until the sauce thickens. Season with salt and lemon pepper to taste. Remove from the heat and add the fried onions, bacon, lardons, garlic and nuts (reserve some nuts to sprinkle on top). Stir in the eggs.

Place the preserved figs randomly over the base of the prepared tart dish and then pour the white sauce mixture over the top. Crumble the cheese on top and sprinkle with the reserved nuts. Bake in the oven for 20–30 minutes. Remove from the oven and allow to cool. Slice and serve at room temperature.

SERVES 4–6

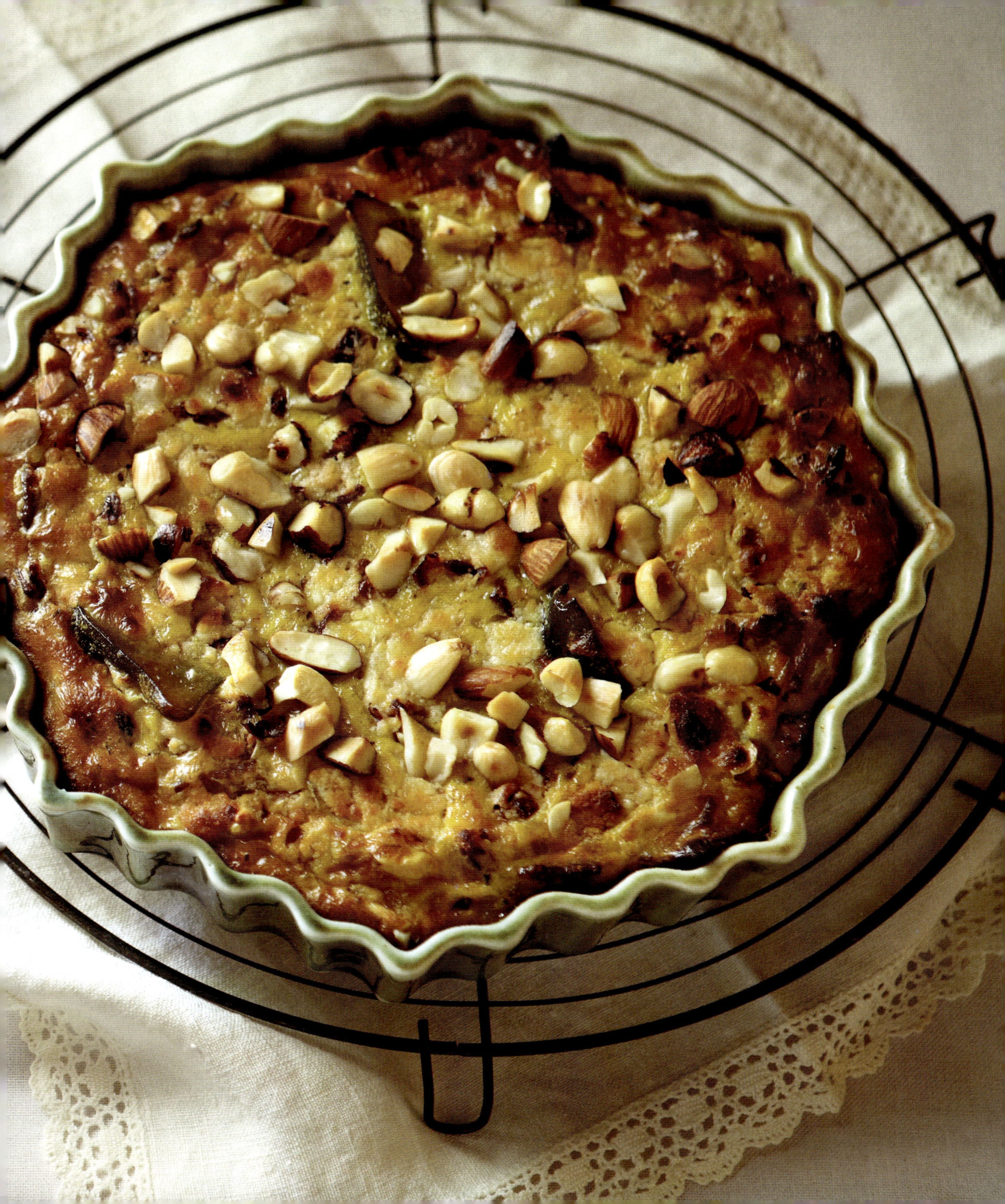

ASG's health bread

This is our famous Andries Stockenström Guest House and Gordon's Restaurant bread recipe. This is just the best health bread and though it may seem a bit of a schlep to make with two separate dough mixtures, the recipe makes enough for three loaves. The bread keeps very well so the extra loaves can be wrapped in plastic wrap and stored in the fridge until you need them, then simply remove the plastic wrap, rewrap in foil and warm in the oven for 10 minutes before slicing the piping hot and super wholesome bread.

If you make two batches, you'll have enough bread for a week. It certainly beats having to run down to the shop every day to buy bread and it's great for school lunches and even better with soup. All our guests love it and so will you.

DOUGH MIX 1

40 g fresh yeast (ask your local bakery)
1 litre tepid water
30 ml oil
30 ml honey
15 ml white grape vinegar
600 g wholewheat flour

DOUGH MIX 2

300 g white bread flour
300 g crushed wheat
100 g sunflower seeds
100 g linseeds
20 ml salt
20 ml brown sugar

Mix all of dough mix 1's ingredients together in a mixing bowl. Cover with a cloth and leave to rise for 10–15 minutes. Once risen, set the oven temperature to 200 °C and grease 3 bread loaf pans.

When the first dough mix has risen, mix it with all the ingredients from dough mix 2. Use a wooden spoon and mix really well.

Divide the dough between the prepared pans and leave to rise again. Once risen, bake for 45 minutes in an electric oven* or 60 minutes for gas.

MAKES 3 LOAVES

* If using an electric oven, place a bowl of water in the oven at the same time to prevent the loaves from drying out.

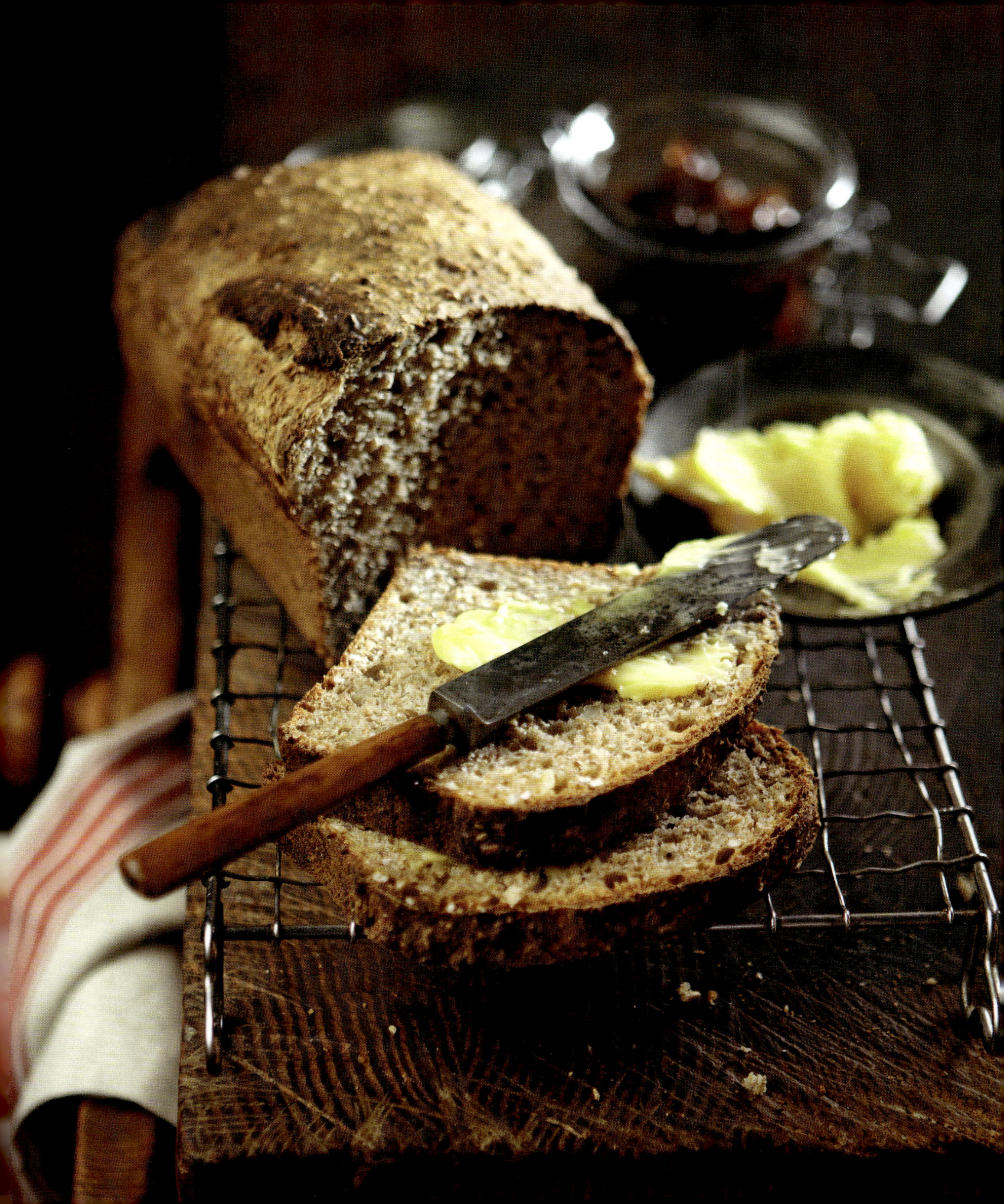

Maryke's baked *pap* tart

Dave and Maryke Stern are great friends of ours. They farm in the mountains near Nieu-Bethesda where it is really chilly in winter, with regular snowfalls. During the summer months, however, Dave and I play country cricket for the Bethesda Road Cricket Club with a bunch of local farmer mates in the country districts league. We all have great fun and don't take the cricket too seriously (in the slips there is often more talk of lucerne harvests and how much rain so-and-so had than actual cricket), and we all enjoy the day out with our families and friends.

Maryke is a real nature girl and absolutely loves the farm life and, of course, cooking in her big old farm kitchen. This recipe makes a nice big batch so make sure you have plenty of mates to share it with. Maybe even your own cricket team.

Olive oil
2 onions, chopped
4 cloves garlic, chopped
2 large tomatoes, chopped
2 sprigs fresh rosemary, chopped
Salt and freshly ground pepper
500 g cooked maize meal (*pap*) or polenta – nice and sloppy
1 can (400 g) whole kernel corn
1 big bunch spinach, chopped
80 g each Cheddar and Gouda cheese, grated

Preheat the oven to 180 °C. Grease a baking tray or deep ovenproof pie dish.

Heat the oil in a frying pan and sweat the onions and garlic until soft and translucent. Add the tomatoes and rosemary, and simmer for 5 minutes until soft. Season to taste.

Layer the *pap*, tomato and onion mix, corn and spinach in the prepared dish. Repeat until all the ingredients are used up, ending with a layer of *pap*. Top off with grated cheese. Bake in the oven, uncovered, for 25 minutes.

Serve with grilled lamb chops and a generous piece of braaied wors.

SERVES 6–8

Marinated prune and chilli salad with pistachio nuts and rocket

We were out visiting some friends one lovely spring day, standing around the braai tanning some chops and having a few beers, when our hostess came out with this amazing looking salad. I couldn't help myself and had to have a taste, and the recipe.

This is such a wonderful summery salad. The rocket gives it a spicy, peppery bite that you just can't get with lettuce. It's also super healthy and looks great on any table.

75 ml olive oil
1 medium red pepper, diced
1 medium yellow pepper, diced
20 ml chopped fresh thyme
15 ml finely chopped chilli
2 cloves garlic, finely chopped
15 ml balsamic vinegar
15 ml sea salt
12 dried prunes*, pitted
50 g shelled, chopped pistachio nuts
50 g rocket

Heat a little of the olive oil in a pan and fry the peppers lightly. Mix with the remaining ingredients, toss lightly and enjoy!

SERVES 6

* If the prunes are a bit sour, add 5–7 ml sugar.

Mini potato bakes

These little potato bakes are brilliant with any dish but particularly awesome for a cold, wintery, comfort food day. They are a smaller version and a slightly different take on the traditional potato bake.

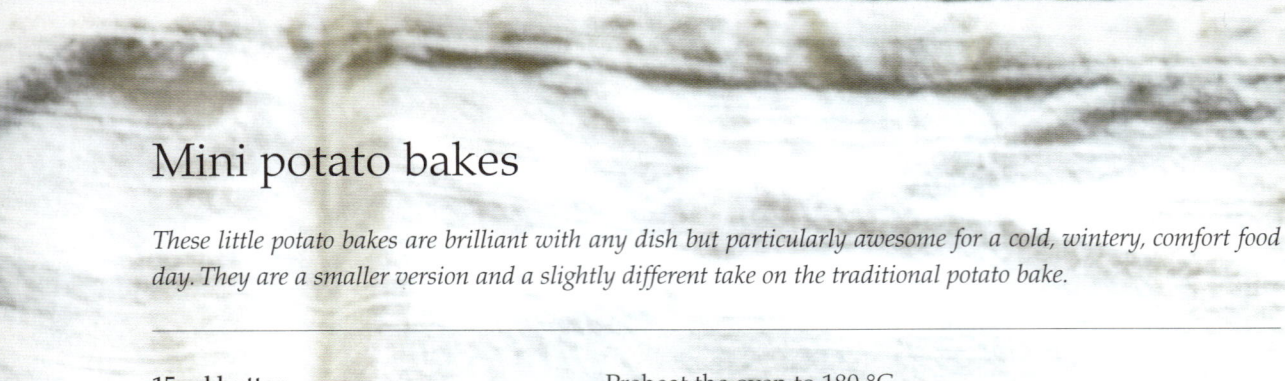

15 ml butter
4 medium potatoes, cooked and thinly sliced
1 onion, very thinly sliced (optional)
125 g Parmesan cheese, grated
250 ml thick cream
Salt and freshly ground pepper

Preheat the oven to 180 °C.

Using four smallish, shallow, pie-type dishes, put a dollop of butter at the bottom of each dish, then add layers of potato, onion (if using), cheese and a dash of cream. Continue layering (don't forget to salt and pepper as you go) until all the dishes are three-quarters full.

Top off with a last dash of cream and the last bit of cheese and pop into the oven for 20 minutes, or until golden on top and bubbling.

Remove from the oven and allow to settle for 2–3 minutes. Loosen the edges with a knife, carefully slide out of the baking dishes and serve immediately.

Scrumptious comfort food.

SERVES 4

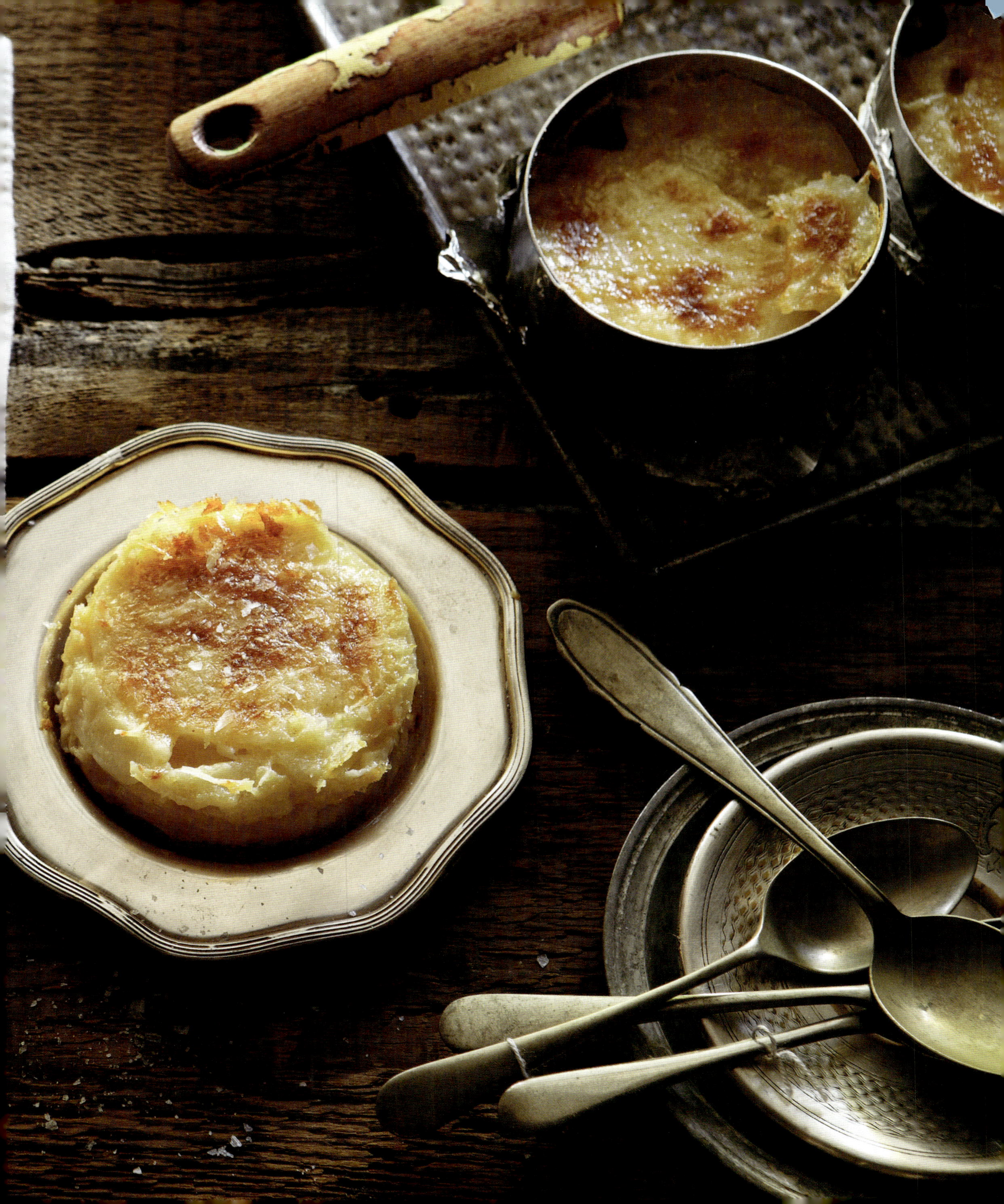

Magic potatoes

I'm not one to brag, but these are quite possibly the most awesome roast potatoes you will ever make. My family call them 'Dad's magic potatoes' and I love making them. They need a little preparation and they absolutely won't be rushed, but they are so worth it.

Make them whenever you are doing a roast* and just pop them into the same roasting pan so they can suck up all those delicious roasting juices or, if you prefer, do them in their own dish.

6 large washed and unpeeled baking potatoes, halved (if you're using baby potatoes, obviously use more)
1 handful coarse sea salt
1 handful cracked black pepper
15 ml mustard powder
125 ml finely chopped fresh rosemary
1 good glug olive oil
50 g butter
10 ml paprika

Cook the potatoes in a large saucepan of boiling, salted water for 10 minutes, or until they are soft for the first 2 cm when pricked with a fork. You only want the outside soft; inside should be hard and firm. Once ready, remove from the heat, drain and allow to steam dry for a few minutes.

Add the rest of the ingredients, except the paprika, to the saucepan, put the lid back on and shake the pot around madly to ensure that all the seasoning coats the potatoes thoroughly and the outer surface is broken up a bit.

Turn out into a preheated roasting dish or place around the already cooking roast, being sure to spoon all the mushy bits from the pot over the potatoes. Drizzle one last glug of olive oil over the top and add a good sprinkling of paprika. Place in the oven, uncovered, and roast until crispy and golden.

If the roast is ready before the potatoes, don't fret, just remove the roast from the pan, give the potatoes a good shake up to loosen them from the bottom of the pan, pour off any excess meat juices, then return them to the oven with the temperature cranked up to around 240 °C. Continue roasting while the meat is resting and you are making the gravy. By the time you are ready, they should be crispy, crunchy, golden and absolutely magic!

SERVES 4–6 (bank on 1 potato per person on average)

* If you want to do them on their own, follow the same procedure as above, but just bake at 180 °C for 45 minutes. Give the potatoes a good shake up, being sure to loosen and turn any that stick to the bottom of the dish and return to the oven for a further 20 minutes at 240 °C, or until golden brown and looking delicious.

Crunchy seasonal veg with butter and salt

I hate mushy vegetables. I think the best veg are slightly soft on the surface but crisp and slightly crunchy in the middle. This side dish is great to showcase how tasty the right mix of veg can be. You could even have it as a main course, if you fancy. I like to use vegetables that are in season and with similar cooking times, such as carrots, baby marrows, broccoli and patty pan squash, but feel free to use whatever you like. Homegrown vegetables are always the best; just make sure you don't overcook them!

3 carrots, quartered lengthways
4 courgettes, quartered lengthways
4 golden patty pan squash, quartered
1 small head broccoli, broken into florets
15 ml butter
Pinch of salt

Place all the veg and 250 ml salted water in a saucepan, and bring to the boil. Allow to boil for about 3 minutes, then pour off the water and turn the heat right down to low. Add the butter, a pinch of salt and stir gently. You want the butter to melt slowly and coat the veg, not fry it.

Once the butter has melted and coated the vegetables, place the lid on the saucepan and simmer gently for about 5 minutes, or until the veg is done to your taste. (Ideally, if you stab a piece of veg with a fork it should slide off without breaking the vegetable apart.) Once ready, serve immediately.

SERVES 4

Seasonal green beans with roasted almonds and crispy bacon

A firm family favourite when the garden is full of beans. The crunchy textures and mixture of bacony nuttiness ensures the kids love it too. Great for a summer's day.

---

500 g green beans, topped
1 dash olive oil
100 g bacon bits
30 g flaked almonds

Pop the beans into a pot of boiling water for 5 minutes.
    Whilst the beans are cooking, heat the olive in a hot pan and fry the bacon bits until crisp. Remove from the pan and set aside.
    Using the same pan, pour off any excess bacon fat, toss in the almond flakes and roast until golden brown. Remove and set aside.
    When the beans are crunchy and three-quarters cooked, remove them from the pot and place in a serving dish. Sprinkle over the bacon and almonds and you're done. (I sometimes add feta too.)

SERVES 4–6

Honey-glazed parsnips

I like to use wild honey from my own bees; it's dark, syrupy and full of the flavours of the veld. Try to get wild honey if you can but if you can't, make sure the honey you use has not been boiled as all the goodness is gone if it has been. Most speciality shops will be able to supply you with good-quality honey.

---

6 large parsnips, peeled and roughly chopped (if small, leave whole or slice in half lengthways)
Olive oil
30 ml honey
1 sprig fresh thyme

Add the parsnips to a saucepan of boiling, salted water and cook for about 20 minutes, or until the parsnips are three-quarters cooked.
    Pour off the water and toss the parsnips into a heavy-based frying pan with a glug of olive oil, the honey and the thyme. Simmer for 5 minutes over low heat, stirring gently until the parsnips are cooked through and thoroughly glazed with the honey. Be sure not to use too much heat because the honey will burn.
    Once done, remove from the heat and serve. Wonderful with most venison dishes.

SERVES 4–6

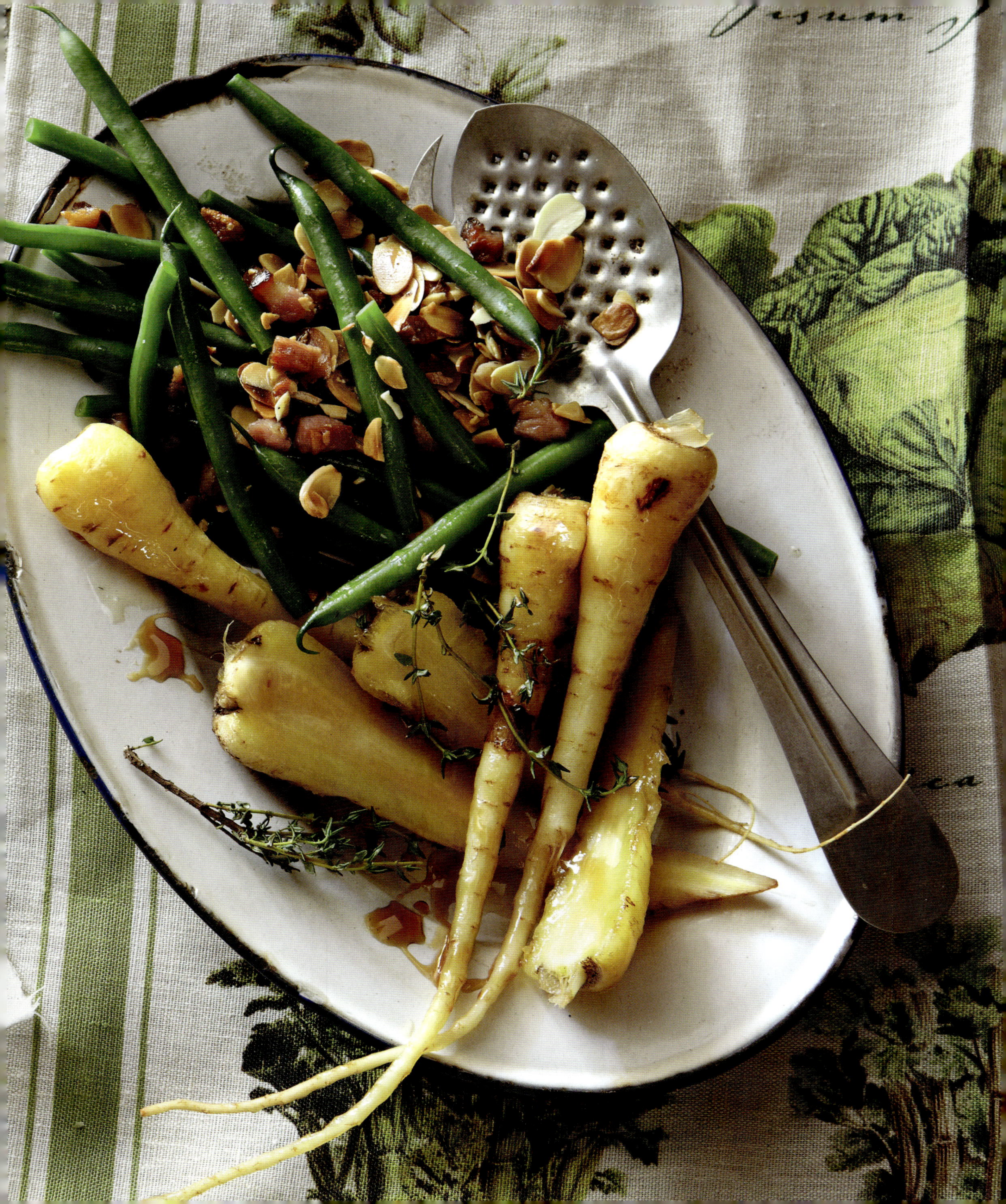

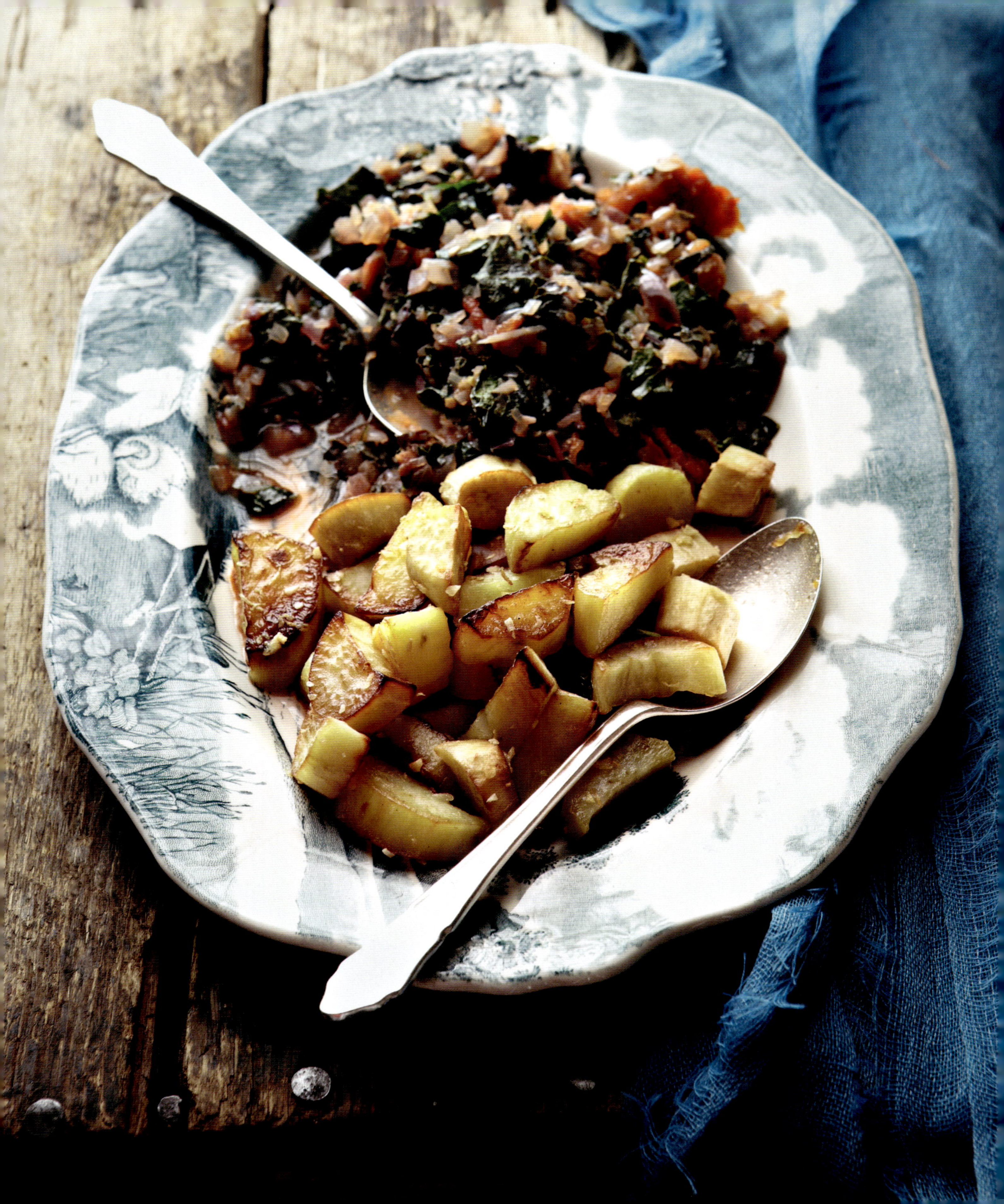

Stir-fried sweet potato with garlic, ginger and coriander

This is a very cool way to add some gusto to the good old sweet potato. It can be served as a side dish at a braai but is also posh enough for a formal dinner. It goes very well with venison and is great with pork and lamb chops.

Be sure to only add the coriander right at the end or else it could overpower the other flavours of the dish. It's traditionally made in a three-legged potjie, but I like to use my wok.

Olive oil
500 g sweet potato, peeled and cut into 5 cm cubes
2 cloves garlic, grated
1 thumb-sized piece fresh ginger, grated
½ handful fresh coriander

Add a glug of olive oil to a hot wok and then stir-fry the sweet potatoes, tossing regularly until the outsides of the cubes are nicely coloured. Reduce the heat to low and add the garlic and ginger. Stir through, put the lid on and simmer for about 20 minutes, tossing occasionally, until the sweet potatoes are soft.

When the cubes are cooked through, remove from the heat, add the coriander and serve straight away.

Splendid!

SERVES 4–6

Traditional morogo (wild African spinach)

Morogo (also called marog) is a type of wild African spinach and is super healthy and tasty. It is such a traditional African dish and out here in the Karoo is no exception. There are so many different ways to prepare it, but this is my favourite. If you can't get real morogo, substitute spinach or Swiss chard.

Olive oil
1 red onion, roughly chopped
2 cloves garlic, chopped
2 large tomatoes, peeled and roughly chopped
300 g morogo leaves, stems removed, roughly chopped

Heat a little olive oil in a heavy-based saucepan and sweat the onion until soft and translucent. Add the garlic and tomatoes and simmer for 5–8 minutes.

Add the morogo and simmer, covered, for a further 10 minutes. Serve immediately.

How simple is that?

SERVES 4

Oak-smoked mash

I serve this as a side dish in the restaurant and it's hugely popular. The smoking gives the mash a natural saltiness and the colour is amazing. It's also not too difficult to make, just be sure to use oak shavings (I have a few old oak wine barrels that I have taken apart and use shavings from these) and check that the kitchen is well ventilated. The method given here for smoking potatoes is aimed at someone who does not have access to a proper smoker. If you do have a smoker, then use that instead.

---

4 large potatoes, peeled and halved
Oak shavings or chips
Knob of butter
50 ml milk (or fresh cream if you really want to be decadent)
1 dash olive oil
1 sprig fresh thyme, chopped

Add the potatoes to a saucepan of boiling, salted water and cook for about 30 minutes, or until cooked. Pour off the water and remove the potatoes. Dry them (this is very important as the smoke will not penetrate if the potatoes are wet) and set aside to cool.

Whilst the potatoes are cooling, take out a wok, ideally a non-Teflon®-based one, and scatter a handful of oak shavings or chips on the bottom. Place a round cake rack above the shavings and ensure there is about 5 cm space between the shavings and the rack. When the potatoes are cool enough to handle, place them on the rack and cover the whole lot tightly with foil, shiny side down. Place on a suitable oven plate and turn up to the hottest setting. When the wok gets up to the correct temperature the shavings/chips will start to smoulder (it only takes about a minute). Reduce the heat by half and allow the potatoes to smoke for about 30 minutes. Don't open the foil lid until right near the end or all the smoke will escape.

The potatoes are ready when they are golden brown. Remove from the wok (be sure to dispose of the ash from the shavings carefully so as not to start a fire) and place into a bowl suitable for mashing. Add the butter, milk, olive oil and thyme to the potatoes and mash until smooth and lump free.

I sometimes spoon the mash into an ovenproof dish, add a sprinkling of Parmesan cheese and paprika on top and pop it into the oven at 180 °C for about 15 minutes.

SERVES 4–6

Roasted beetroot with feta and fresh mint

This bright pink side dish is a delicious way to dress up the oft' forgotten beetroot. I get my feta from my old mate and dairy farmer Tim Murray at Roodebloem farm just outside Graaff-Reinet, but if you can't get any from Tim, just pop down to your local store instead. This dish is great with roasted lamb or chicken.

2–3 medium beetroot, trimmed and scrubbed
Salt and freshly ground pepper
190 ml whipped cream
2 sprigs fresh mint
1 clove garlic, crushed
125 ml crumbled feta cheese
25 ml chopped fresh mint

Preheat the oven to 200 °C.

Place the beetroot in a small baking dish and add enough water to reach about 1 cm up the sides of the dish. Season with salt and pepper, cover the dish with foil and bake for about 45 minutes until the beetroot is soft and tender.

When cooked, remove the beetroot from the oven, carefully remove the foil and set aside to cool. When cooled, peel the beetroot and cut into 1 cm-thick slices. Cover and refrigerate (this can be done in advance).

When you are ready to put the dish together, preheat the oven to 220 °C.

Place the cream, mint sprigs and garlic in a small saucepan and bring to a simmer. Just before it comes to the boil, remove from the heat, cover and let it steep for about 15 minutes.

Grease a shallow baking dish. Layer the beetroot slices in the dish, seasoning each layer lightly with salt. Pour the cream mixture over the beetroot slices and sprinkle the feta cheese over the top.

Bake for about 20 minutes until the cream is bubbling and the feta is lightly browned. Grind over some pepper and sprinkle with the chopped mint. Set aside for 5 minutes before serving.

Lovely and summery.

SERVES 4

Soda Bread

There is no yeast in this bread. 500 g flour, (or ½ and wholemeal mixed, which is very good) 5 ml salt, 5 ml cream of tartar, 5 ml bicarbonate soda, 30 g fat, approximately 250 ml buttermilk or sour milk.

Sieve the dry ingredients into a basin and rub in the fat. Make a well in the centre and mix in enough of the liquid to make a soft, spongy dough. Turn on to a lightly-floured board and shape quickly into 2 round cakes. Place on a floured baking sheet, or tin, and score the top of each loaf three times with a knife. Bake in a fairly hot oven of about 205 degrees C for about 35 minutes, until well risen and only lightly browned. It must be firm underneath.

Grootzeekoegat
Molteno
1980

Dessert in the desert

Almost everyone likes a little bit of sweetness now and again. My wife Rose and the boys, Jason and Max, love to end a meal with a little pud. We often turn the pudding-making into a family affair, with Rose and I doing the legwork and the boys licking the bowls and spoons afterwards as the quality control specialists.

As we live in a semi-arid region that is swelteringly hot in summer and freezing cold in winter, I have a selection of cool and refreshing, as well as warm and comforting, desserts to help you cater for any occasion.

Have fun and, above all, have pud!

Rum and raisin parfait

This is great summer variation of the usual ice cream. You can substitute fresh vanilla for the rum and raisins if you want a more delicate flavour. I like the classic rum and raisin taste, but go ahead and make both and see which one you prefer.

8 egg yolks
250 ml warm sugar syrup*
100 g raisins
35 ml rum
250 ml fresh cream, whipped

Whisk the egg yolks and add them to the warm sugar syrup. Heat slowly for 5 minutes, stirring continuously, but don't let it boil.
    Remove from the heat and add the raisins. Set aside until completely cool.
    Add the rum and the whipped cream and stir together until well mixed. Pour into a freezerproof container (or containers) and freeze overnight.

MAKES ENOUGH FOR ABOUT 6 SERVINGS

* Sugar syrup: to get 250 ml syrup, you need 600 ml water and 200 g sugar. Boil and allow to reduce to a thick syrup.

Baked almond creams

These are similar to sweet soufflés. The almond nuttiness has a delicate flavour that works so well for me and I like to fill them with fresh berries, slices of fresh fig or even chocolate and bake them in little muffin pans. Serve piping hot on a cool evening.

100 g butter
100 g sugar
200 g almonds, finely crushed
6 eggs
75 ml rum
Filling ingredients of choice, such as berries, chocolate, figs etc.

Preheat the oven to 170 °C. Grease a muffin pan.
    Cream the butter and sugar together and then add the almonds.
    Add the eggs, one at a time, beating well after each addition. Add the rum and mix well.
    Place a small scoop of mixture into 8–10 of the muffin pan recesses, just enough to cover the bottom. Add your favourite filling and then place another scoop of the almond mixture on top. Be sure to fill the pans to only halfway as everything rises during baking (like a soufflé) and you don't want it cooking over into your oven.
    Bake for 10–15 minutes until the tops are browned and everything has risen nicely. Remove from the oven and pop out of the pans gently (you may need to ease them out with a knife). Serve immediately.

MAKES 8–10 SMALLISH PORTIONS

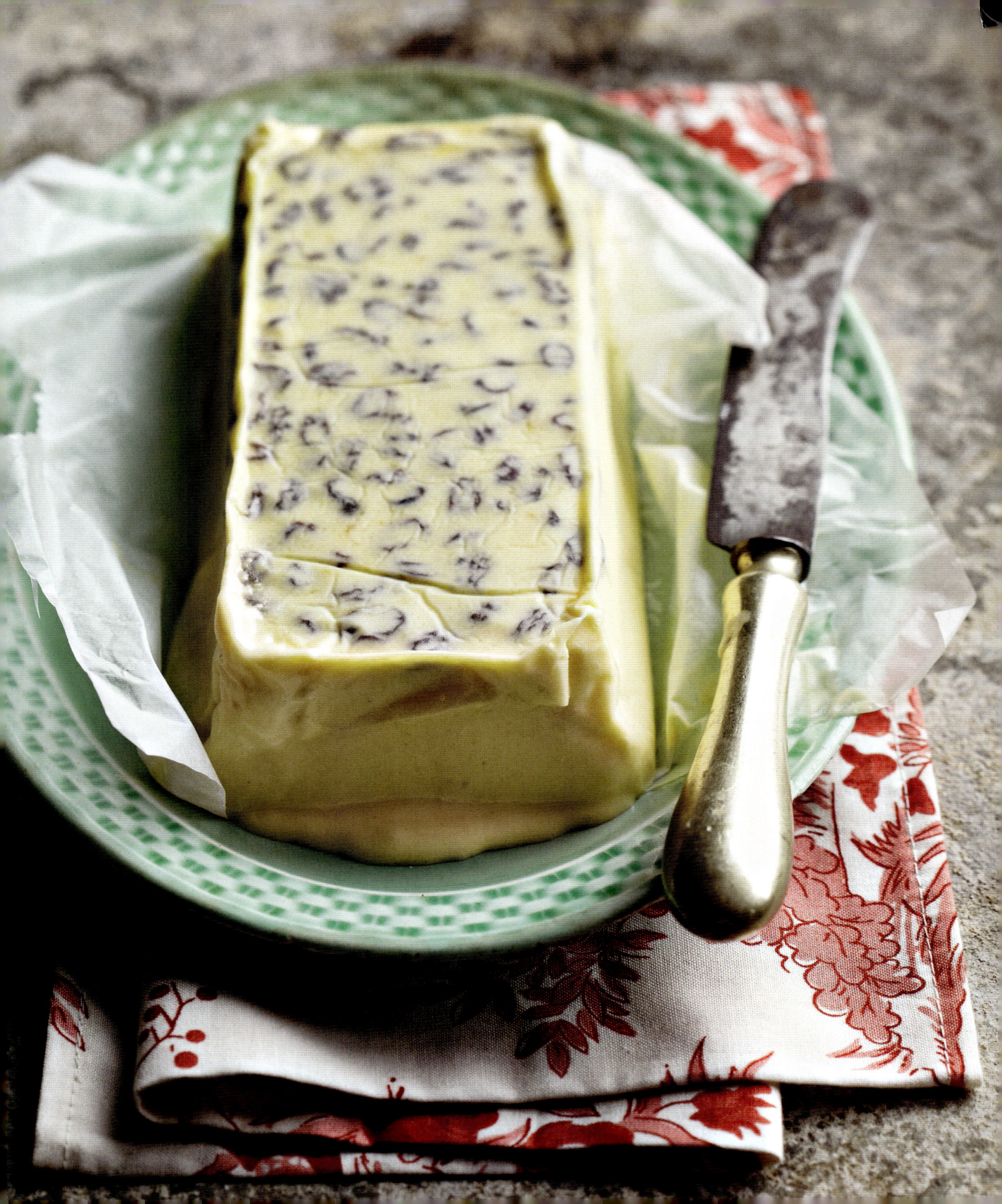

3/4 cup sugar
1/4 cup butter
2 cups Flour
1 egg
3/4 cup hot milk
1 teaspoon bicarb
3/4 cup bananas
1 teaspoon Baking
mix and bake

Decadent chocolate and coffee soufflés

I love this rich and dark decadence. The recipe is as old as the hills but it remains a firm favourite, particularly when served with a good Pinotage.

2 large eggs, separated, plus 2 large egg whites, at room temperature
120 ml granulated sugar
60 ml unsweetened cocoa
15 ml coffee liqueur, such as Kahlúa, or coffee syrup
5 ml vanilla extract
6 chocolate truffles, about 5 cm in diameter (I like to use Lindor balls or even Ferrero Rocher)

Preheat the oven to 190 °C. Butter six 180 ml soufflé dishes, ramekins or custard cups. Coat each with some sugar, tapping out the excess.

In a small bowl, beat or whisk the 2 egg yolks with 30 ml of the sugar for about 3 minutes until pale and thickened. Whisk in the cocoa, liqueur and vanilla.

In a large mixing bowl, beat the 4 egg whites to soft peak stage using an electric mixer. Gradually add the remaining 90 ml sugar and beat to firm peaks.

Fold the cocoa mixture into the egg whites. Divide amongst the prepared dishes and fill to about one-quarter full. Place a truffle in each dish. Fill to halfway and then place on a baking tray. Don't overfill as they still need to puff up to at least double their size.

Bake the soufflés for 15–20 minutes until well puffed. Serve immediately with a glass of good Pinotage.

SERVES 6

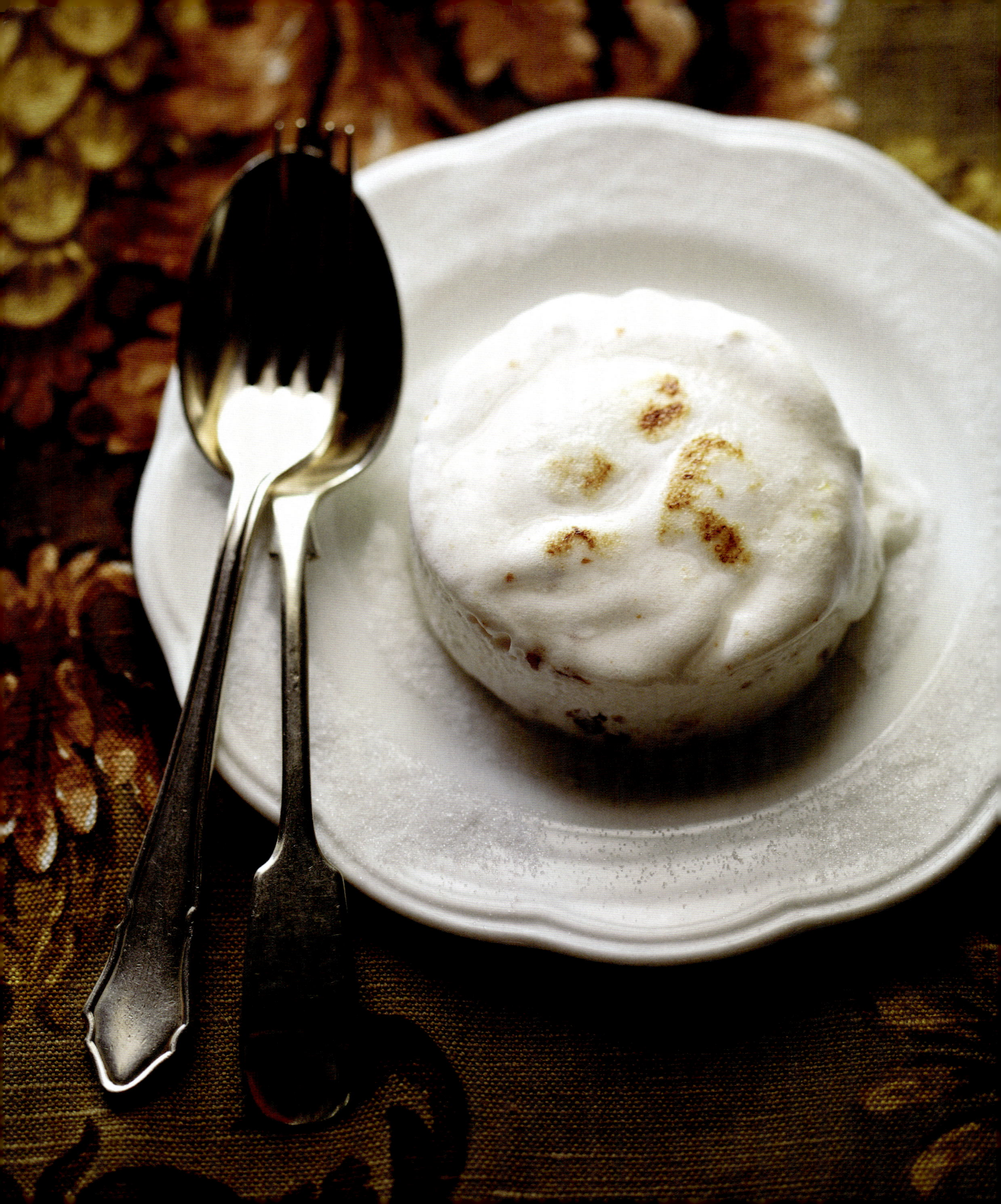

Frozen hazelnut nougat

This cold dessert is one of my favourites of all time: rich, crunchy and decadent yet beautifully soft, smooth and sort of ice creamy. I like to offset the sweetness with granadilla (passion fruit) because the tartness contrasts and yet complements this dessert perfectly. You need to make this in three separate parts and then blend them together.

CARAMELISED HAZELNUTS
80 g castor sugar
80 g hazelnuts

NOUGAT
6 egg whites
250 g castor sugar
2.5 ml vanilla essence
375 ml fresh cream

Part 1: To make the caramelised hazelnuts, place the sugar in a heavy-based pan and heat. Add the hazelnuts and mix until the nuts are caramelised and the mixture is a beautiful golden colour. Pour onto a heat-resistant surface (be very careful as this mixture is incredibly hot and can easily burn you quite badly if spilled). Set aside and allow to cool completely.

Part 2: To make the nougat, whisk the egg whites and the castor sugar together in a double boiler. Whisk continuously until the mixture is warm and fluffy. Remove from the heat, add the vanilla and whisk until cool but still fluffy.

Part 3: Roughly crush the caramelised hazelnuts with a meat mallet or suitable bashing device. Whisk the cream until stiff.

Fold the whipped cream and caramelised hazelnuts into the egg white mixture and mix well.

Pour into freezerproof containers (you can use old ice-cream containers) and freeze overnight.

Serve big scoops as is on a hot sunny day or add a spoonful of granadilla pulp on top. You'll be the most popular person in the neighbourhood.

SERVES 6–8

Malva pudding

A South African and Karoo winter favourite, often imitated but never beaten, this is one of the original recipes that the Voortrekkers used. It is simple, straightforward and sooo good; I don't really see why you would want to do anything different.

10 ml apricot jam (preferably homemade)
10 ml butter
250 ml sugar
1 egg
250 ml cake flour
250 ml milk
5 ml baking powder
10 ml grape vinegar
250 ml fresh cream

SYRUP
125 ml water
250 ml sugar
250 g butter

Preheat the oven to 180 °C.

Mix the jam, butter, sugar and egg together until combined. Add the flour, milk, baking powder and vinegar. Mix well and then pour into a well-greased ovenproof dish. Bake for about 30 minutes.

To make the syrup, heat the water, sugar and butter together in a saucepan over low heat until the butter has melted and the sugar has dissolved.

When the pudding comes out the oven after 30 minutes, pour over half of the syrup and return the pudding to the oven for another 10 minutes. Remove from the oven and pour over the fresh cream. Bake again for 10 minutes.

Pour the remaining syrup* over the pudding and ENJOY!

SERVES 4–6

* I usually prepare the pudding in advance and save the last half of the syrup until shortly before serving. Pour it over and pop into the oven for 10 minutes.

Rose's winter comfort orange pudding

Rose makes this on winter days when the boys come home from school, frozen stiff and half starving to death, their fingers and toes as chilled as their mood. When they walk in and smell that orangey aroma, however, everything changes and great excitement ensues. By the end of lunch, spirits are cheered and hearts are warmed. Life can continue with a smile. That's the power of pudding.

80 g butter
240 g sugar
4 eggs, separated (egg whites beaten until stiff)
60 ml cake flour
Grated rind and juice of 1 orange
500 ml milk

Preheat the oven to 180 °C. Grease an ovenproof dish.

Cream the butter and sugar together. Add the egg yolks and beat thoroughly. Add the flour, orange rind and juice, and then add the milk. Lastly fold in the stiffly beaten egg whites (the stiffer the egg whites the lighter your pudding will be). Pour the mixture into the dish, place it a roasting pan (or similar) and add hot water until it comes halfway up the sides of the pudding dish.

Bake for 45–60 minutes. Because this pudding has a light cake topping with an orange curd-type sauce underneath, it often does not look cooked. Don't worry, simply switch off the oven and leave the dish inside for a while until the pudding has settled. Serve with fresh cream or homemade ice cream.

SERVE 4–6

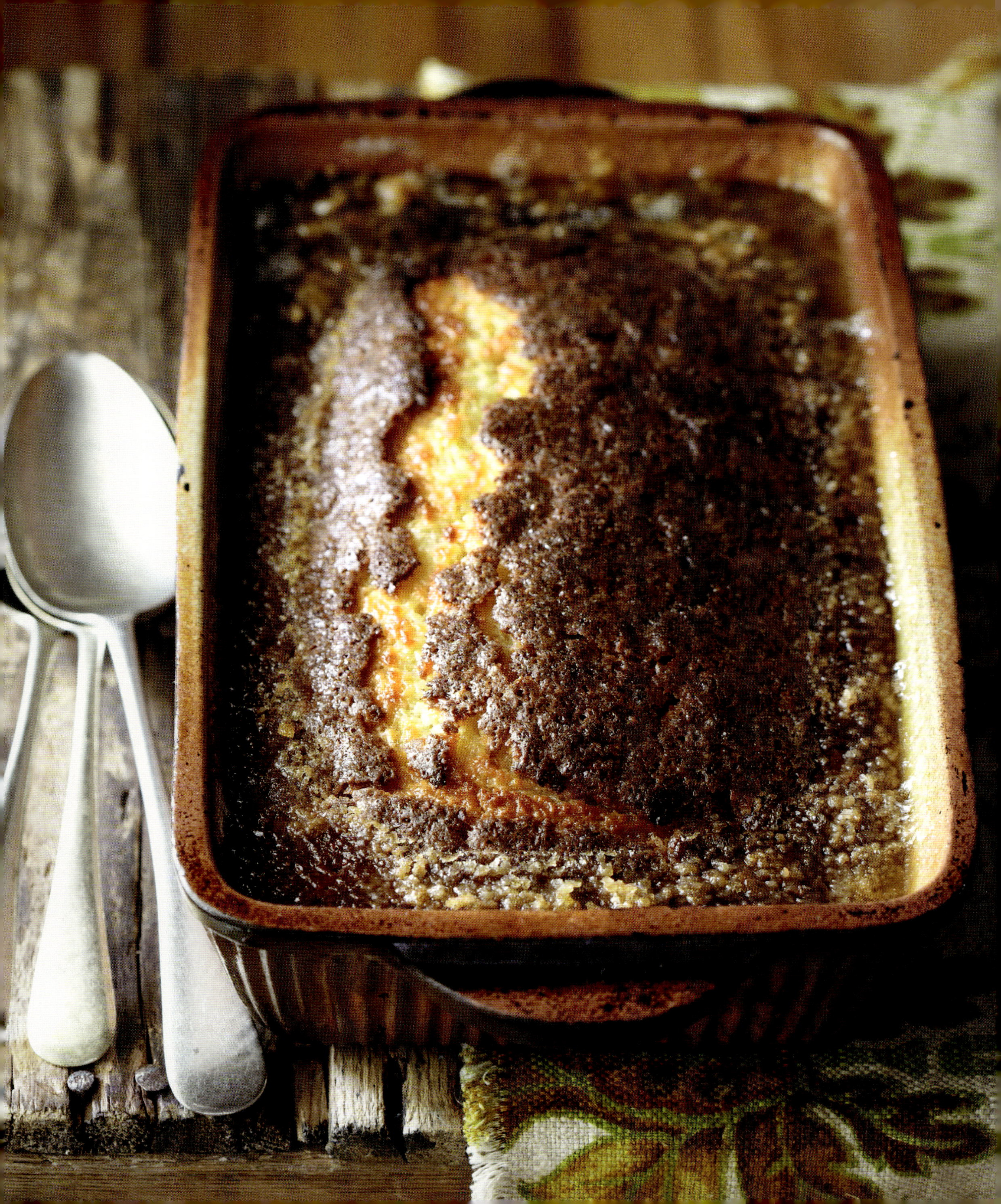

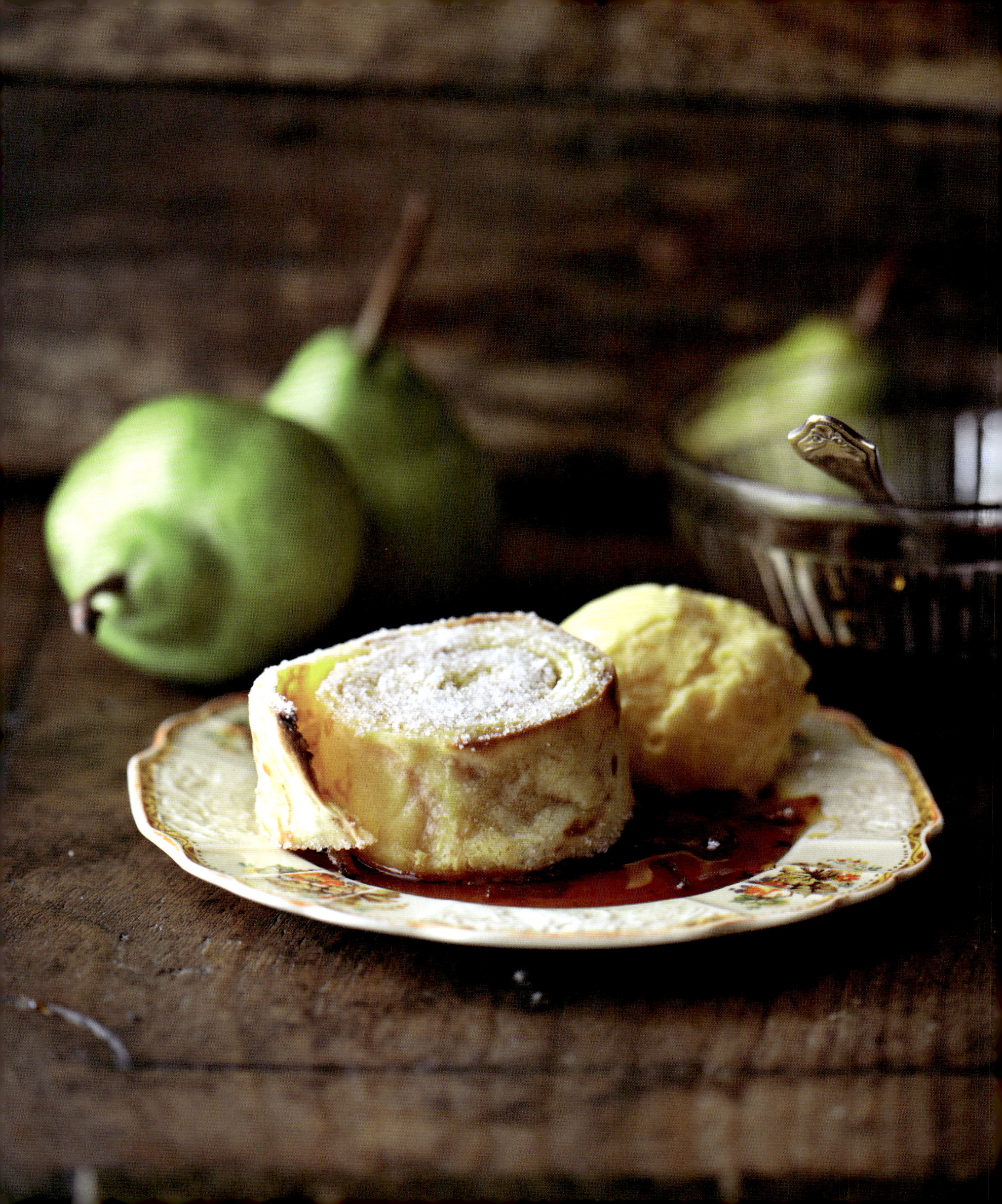

Baked pancake roll with pear and brandy sauce

As I tell my restaurant guests when describing this decadent dessert, this is the sort of pancake you are highly unlikely to find at your local church bazaar. It is quite complicated to make initially, but once you get it right you will see that it's actually rather brilliant and not as tricky as it first seems. You can also store the pancake roll in the freezer and take out and cut off as much as you need, dependent on how many people you have around. Once again, there are three parts to this recipe and all need to be prepared individually before combining them. The bonus here is that you can do the prep work well in advance and just put everything together quickly at the last minute for a really showy dessert.

PEAR AND BRANDY SAUCE
125 ml sugar
2 hard pears, sliced (not too thin; about the thickness of Grandpa's thumb nail!)
180 ml good brandy

PANCAKES
300 g cake flour
Pinch of salt
120 g sugar
6 eggs
650 ml milk
65 ml brandy
200 ml fresh cream

PANCAKE FILLING
300 ml milk
85 g cake flour
135 g sugar
Pinch of salt
10 ml cold butter
2 eggs, whisked

Part 1: To make the pear sauce, caramelise the sugar in a heavy-based saucepan until golden brown. Add the pear slices and stir gently to ensure the slices don't break. Once mixed together, add the brandy and simmer for 5–8 minutes until the sauce becomes syrupy. Set aside.

Part 2: To make the pancakes, sift the cake flour, salt and sugar together. Whisk the eggs well and add 60 ml of the milk. Add the brandy. Slowly add the cake flour and then add the rest of the milk and the cream. Whisk together until the batter is the consistency of thickish cream. Once the batter is ready, make batches of thin pancakes in a suitable pan and set aside to cool.

Part 3: To make the filling, gently heat the milk (don't let it boil!). Mix all the dry ingredients together and grate the butter into the mixture. Mix well. Slowly add the warm milk. Add the eggs and heat the mixture gently in a double boiler, stirring continuously until creamy and thick. Set aside to cool.

Right, now comes the fun part. Place one cooled pancake on a large sheet of plastic wrap (about 30 x 40 cm). Spread a thin layer of the cooled pancake filling on top, then add another pancake and another layer of filling. Repeat until you have a stack of pancakes about 10 cm high. Carefully roll into a tight long roll, similar to a Swiss roll. Cut off the ends to give it a uniform shape, wrap tightly in the plastic wrap and set aside. Continue doing this until you have used all the pancakes and the filling and have a couple of rolls. Refrigerate the rolls you want to use that day and freeze the spares for another time.

When ready to assemble the dessert, preheat the oven to 180 °C.

Remove the pancake rolls from the fridge once they have set and remove the plastic wrap. Slice into the required number of portions and lay them flat on a greased baking tray. Sprinkle with a little castor sugar and bake for about 15 minutes until the edges go all brown and crispy, and the top is caramelised.

Gently reheat the pear and brandy sauce and place a dollop on each plate. When the pancakes are done, remove from the oven and place a slice on each dollop of sauce. Top off with a scoop of ice cream and serve immediately with a look on your face that says 'Please people, I do this every day!'.

MAKES ENOUGH FOR 4–6 PEOPLE

CHAPTER XIII.—PRESERVING

Leave over night—
Add a spoon tablespoon Turpentine

CHAPTER XIII.
PRESERVING.
INTRODUCTION.

All putrefaction is due to the presence of germs in the food. Therefore all methods of preserving aim at excluding these germs, rendering them inactive, or entirely destroying them.

To flourish, and cause putrefaction in the food the germs require warmth and moisture.

Preservation of food is therefore brought about in one of the following ways:—

(a) By destroying all germs by heat, as sterilising or preserving fruit in syrup.
(b) By excluding air and germs altogether as preserved eggs.
(c) By depriving the germs of warmth as in cold storage treatment.
(d) By depriving the germs of moisture as in drying of biltong, mushrooms, fruit, etc.
(e) By treating with an antiseptic as vinegar, as pickles, chutneys, etc., and also sugar, as jams, and salt in curing.
(f) By a combination of some of the above methods.

The following methods and recipes will show the various applications of this general principle.

CONTENTS OF THIS CHAPTER.

I. The Fruits of South Africa.
II. Jams.
III. Marmalades.
IV. Jellies.
V. Bottled Fruits.
VI. Confôtes, Preserves and Crystallised Fruit.
VII. The Vegetables of South Africa.
VIII. Bottled Vegetables.
IX. Preserved Meats, Game, Soup, etc.
X. Pickles.
XI. Sauces, Ketchups, etc.
XII. Miscellaneous.

---

basin ... an enamel
soda
Melt fat.
When fat is like warm stir soda in.

Preserves
and baked treats

We sometimes have too much of something in the kitchen and don't know what to do with it or would love to have some tasty, ready-to-eat snacks that are healthy and good for the kids. I often have too many chillies or too much basil from the garden, or a farmer friend drops off a couple of boxes of onions too many. Rather than let them go to waste, we make these into tasty preserves and things that can be stored until we need them.

Here are a few ideas to keep everyone happy and the larder stocked up with all sorts of lovely little tasties and, of course, a treat or two.

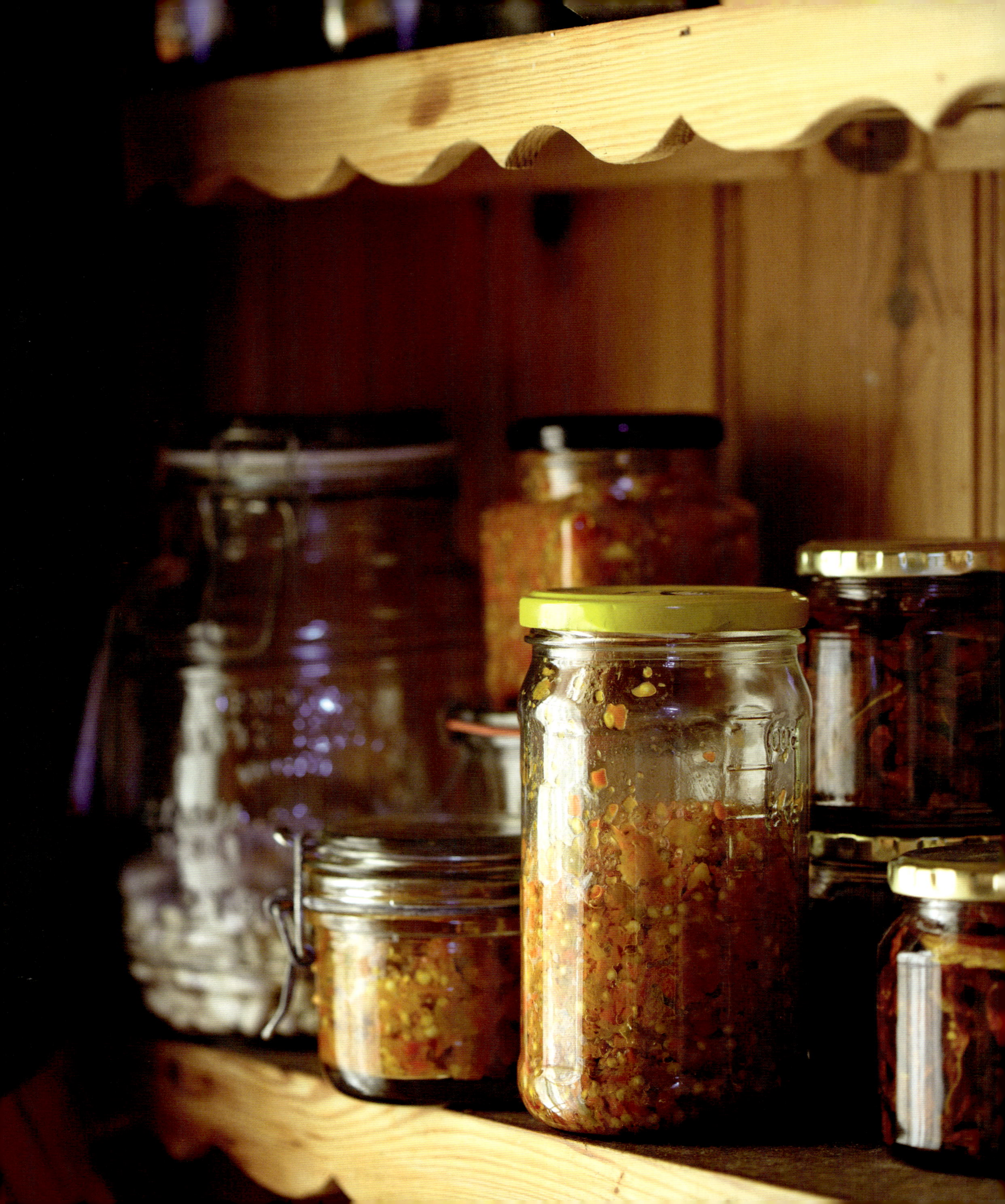

Wonder salt

This stuff is truly magic. Whenever you're cooking a dish and need something to lift the flavour or seem to be missing something but can't think what it is, wonder salt is the answer. Just add a teaspoon, a dash or a pinch to virtually anything and you will be amazed. I call it wonder salt because all your friends will wonder what you put into the dish to make it taste so fantastic. It'll be our little secret …

225 g coarse salt
50 g black peppercorns
100 ml (15 g) ground cloves
150 ml (25 g) ground nutmeg
100 ml (15 g) ground cinnamon
100 ml (15 g) dried basil
100 ml (15 g) ground mace
100 ml (15 g) coriander seeds
3 bay leaves

Mix all the ingredients together, place in a blender and blend to a fine consistency, much like icing sugar.

Store in an airtight container next to the stove and use as necessary, remembering that a little goes a long way.

MAKES ABOUT 375 G

Natalie's lekker-hot bottled chilli relish

I got this great and easy relish recipe from Natalie Erasmus, who farms in the district with her hubby Neil. When chillies are in season, make this hot and spicy relish to add to just about any dish to which you want to give a little zing. I like to use jalapeños as they are full of flavour and have a good but not over-the-top burn. If you are really brave, try bird's-eye chillies. They'll really clean your clock. It keeps for up to 6 months unopened. Do refrigerate after opening and eat within a month

375 ml oil (I use olive oil, but any quality cooking oil will do)
40 ml garlic and ginger paste
750 g chillies, chopped with seeds
250 g chopped onions
5 ml salt
About 250 ml brown vinegar

Heat a little of the oil and fry the garlic and ginger paste for a few seconds. Add the rest of the ingredients, including the remaining oil, and simmer gently over medium heat for about 12 minutes, or until the oil becomes light green in colour.

Bottle in sterilised glass jars and top up with a little oil. If you want a stronger, smoother paste, then place the cooked mixture in the blender and whizz to the desired consistency before bottling.

MAKES ABOUT 3 X 500 ML JARS

Mom's delicious pecan, apricot and peach conserve

One Christmas Eve a few years ago my mom sent me this email:
Gordon my darling lad, I've just made the most delicious concoction that I'm calling 'Pecan, Apricot and Peach Conserve'. I bought myself some apricots and cling peaches recently, but before I could even eat half of them they were ripe. So I decided to invent something nice. I had some cherries left over from the Christmas cake, but they'd got pretty dried-out and sugary, so I made a syrup of my special vanilla sugar (keep vanilla pods in a sealed tub of sugar), a pinch of salt and about a litre or so of water, popped quartered cherries and quartered pecans in this and simmered it till it thickened up nicely. Then I added a lemon leaf and a couple of lemon balm leaves, and added the cling peaches I'd cut into eighths and soaked in port and let them simmer till they were soft and opaque. Then I added the halved apricots and let this simmer for about 6 or so minutes – the apricots very quickly get mushy, so watch them. And then bottled them. But removed the greenery! Got 4 small jars of the conserve and also a small bottle of syrup that I'll use on ice cream! Will have the fruity ones served on a cake base, with cream or ice cream (or even Greek yoghurt) anyway, some such topping, for a pudding. I astonished myself at how nice it is, and depending on your tastes and requirements you can use all sorts of alcoholic beverages. I will possibly try this with other fruits like apples, berries and dried cake fruits as well. Sometimes I astonish myself. Have a good and enjoyable dinner tonight, and tomorrow. Then I trust you'll be able to relax on Monday. Love to Rose and the boys. May you be truly blessed with the Love, Peace and Joy of Christ this Christmas, and may God grant you all a sufficiency of His Health and Richness in the year ahead. All my dear love, Mom.

Though the restaurant and guesthouse were super busy with Christmas bookings, the recipe sounded brilliant and very Christmassy so I tried it out. I served it over plain yoghurt the next morning with breakfast and it was a hit! I then used some in one of my baked desserts with dinner – a hit again! Ever since, I have been using my (slightly edited) version of this conserve in so many dishes. Here it is.

---

1 litre water
100 g vanilla sugar (see email above)
Pinch of salt
Zest of ½ lemon
100 g glazed red cherries
100 g pecan nuts, roughly chopped
500 g apricots, pitted and cut into eighths
500 g cling peaches, pitted, cut into eighths and soaked overnight in port to cover
1 lemon leaf
1 bay leaf
1 cinnamon stick

Pour the water into a saucepan and add the vanilla sugar, salt, lemon zest, cherries and pecans. Bring to the boil, then reduce the heat and simmer for 20 minutes until the pecans are soft and opaque. Add the apricots, drained peaches (reserve the port) and balance of ingredients and simmer for 1 hour, or until the fruit is soft and sticky. (I like to cook it down to a mushy consistency, but cook it for as long as you want, dependant on how mushy you want it.)

Remove from the heat and stir in the port. Using a wooden spoon, ladle into sterilised bottles and seal. (Don't forget to remove the 'greenery', i.e. lemon and bay leaves and cinnamon stick. There will be some syrup left, which you can use as my mother directed or at your own discretion. (Always listen to your mother …)

If you are making this over the Christmas season, Merry Christmas! If not, well happy, happy anyway!

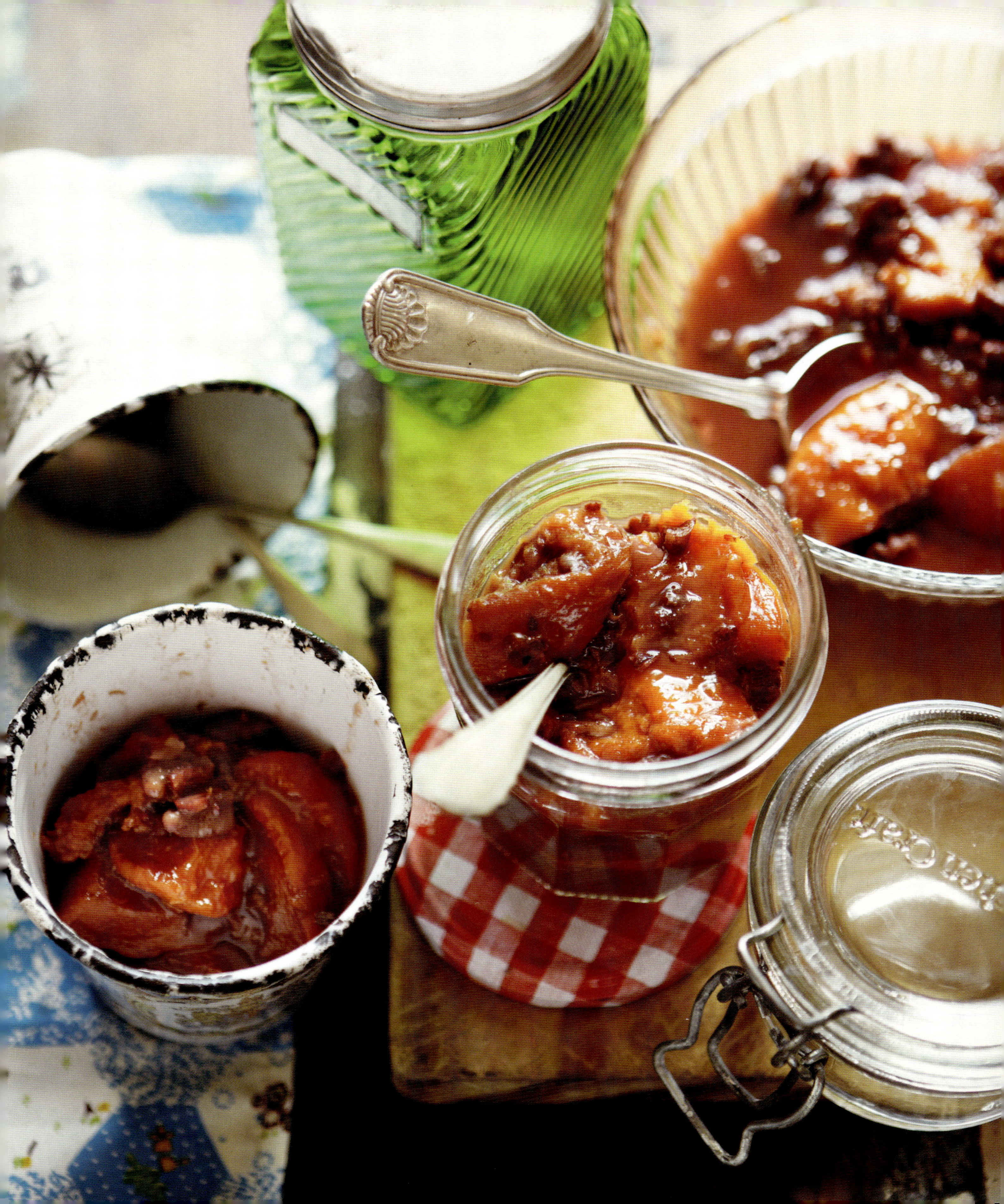

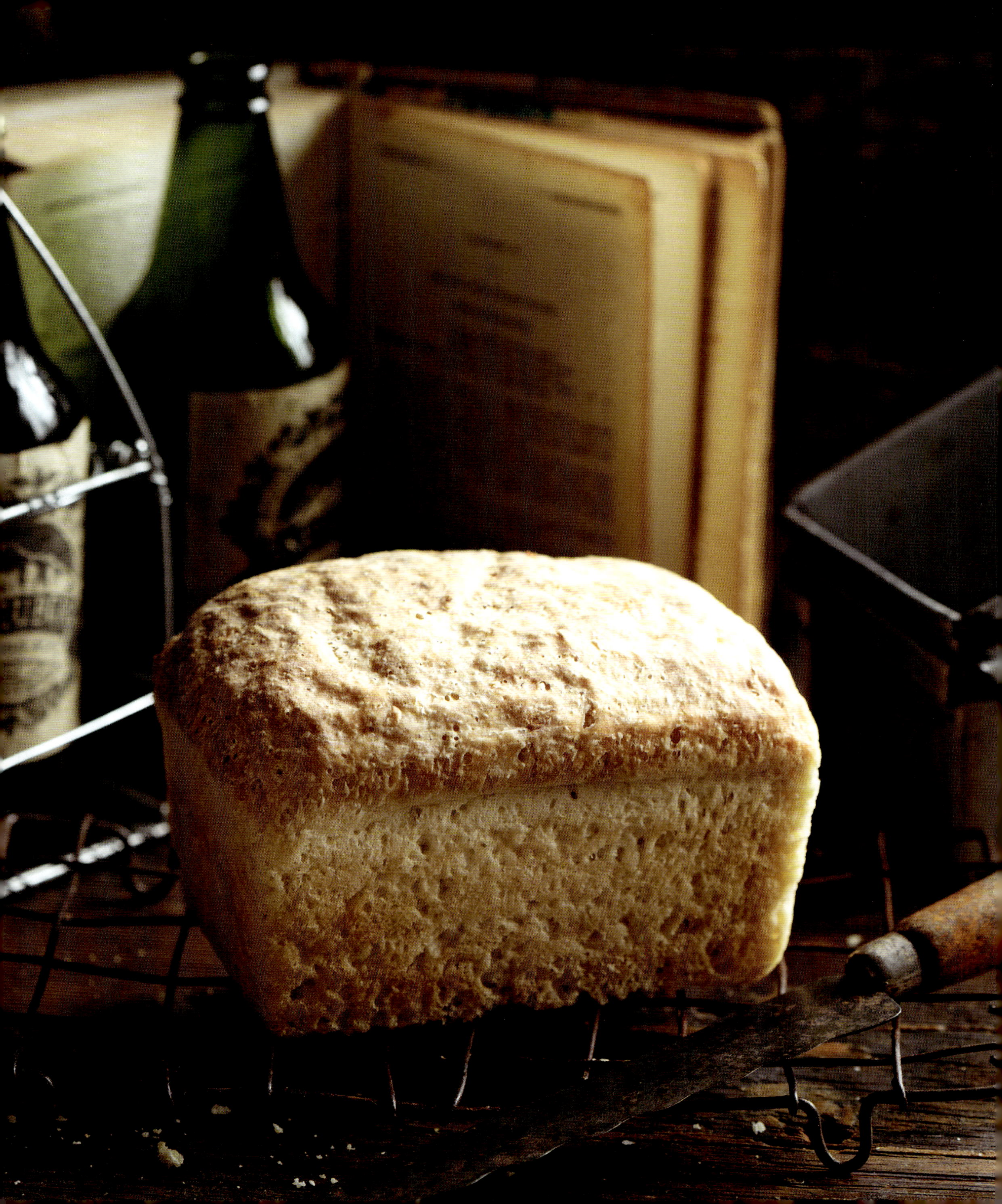

Easy veldbraai beer bread

I make this a lot when out hunting because it's a quick and easy lunchtime snack out in the veld. The addition of cake flour makes the bread a little lighter and fluffier. And don't worry about the alcohol in the beer, it cooks away; you just need the yeast from the beer to act as a raising agent. This bread rises best when placed on a Land Rover fender, parked in the veld on a sunny winter's morning whilst you are out hunting. For the home baker, however, the extra yeast will be necessary. The recipe makes one smallish loaf, enough to feed 4. If you need more, just double up on the recipe and increase the baking time by about two-thirds.

250 g bread flour
250 g cake flour
1 can (340 ml) beer
5 ml salt
1 sachet (10 g) dry yeast (optional)

Combine all the ingredients and mix well until a soft dough is formed. Allow to rise until doubled in size and then bake in a greased flat-bottomed cast-iron pot over the coals (put 5–8 coals on the lid and around 10 underneath the pot) until golden on top and you hear a hollow sound when you tap the bread with your finger.

Turn out and allow to cool while wrapped in a tea towel. Enjoy with butter and apricot jam.

Cara McEwan's *mielie pap* biscuits

One of Rose's best friends, Cara and her husband John farm cattle out near Tarkastad, about 2½ hours' drive northeast of us. They have a wonderful big homestead and Cara loves to bake. She gave this recipe to Rose a few years ago (I think Cara first got it from her mom or mom-in-law) and it is so easy to make.

Whenever we go away on a family holiday, Rose bakes tins and tins of these biscuits for the trip – the kids live on them and I love them with my morning cuppa. We even bake them for the guesthouse.

250 ml cake flour
125 ml maize meal (*mielie pap*)
60 ml bran
Pinch of salt
250 ml white sugar
10 ml baking powder
125 g butter
1 egg

Preheat the oven to 200 °C.

Mix all the ingredients together. Roll the dough into balls the size of walnuts. Place well apart from one another on a baking tray and flatten slightly with the palm of your hand.

Bake for 15 minutes until lightly browned. Transfer to a wire rack to cool and then munch away.

MAKES APPROXIMATELY 40 BISCUITS PER BATCH

Aunty Maureen's marvellous muffins

Aunty Maureen Jacobus – I call her my 'Kitchen General' – has been working at the guesthouse for around 20 years. She has never worked anywhere else in her life and happily stayed on when we took over. She is unbelievably knowledgeable despite no formal training in the kitchen, and is typical of the Karoo women who seem to have a natural cookbook embedded somewhere deep in their genetic make-up.

Maureen makes our world-famous muffins that are not only super tasty hot out of the oven, but are also really healthy and wholesome and make a wonderful mid-morning snack. If you don't believe me, try them for yourself and you'll see.

375 ml finely grated carrots
375 ml grated apples or pears
125 ml sultanas
160 ml desiccated coconut
30 ml sunflower seeds
250 ml oil
5 ml vanilla essence
500 ml cake flour
250 ml sugar
10 ml bicarbonate of soda
10 ml ground cinnamon
Pinch of salt

Preheat the oven to 180 °C. Grease a muffin pan.

Mix the grated carrots and apples with the sultanas, coconut, seeds, oil and vanilla essence.

Mix the flour, sugar, bicarbonate of soda, cinnamon and salt together. Add this mixture to the carrot mixture and mix until only just combined.

Spoon the mixture into the muffin pan and bake for 25–30 minutes.

MAKES ABOUT 6 STANDARD-SIZED MUFFINS OR 12 MINI ONES

Simple summer salad cream

An easy, fresh salad cream to put on anything you fancy. It keeps quite well, but it's so tasty that it usually doesn't last too long anyway.

1 large cucumber, peeled and deseeded
500 ml plain yoghurt
2 large cloves garlic
50 ml white balsamic vinegar
60 ml olive oil
1 good handful fresh mint (or any other herb you fancy – I quite love thyme too)
Salt and freshly ground pepper

Toss all the ingredients into a blender and whizz it all up. Pop it into a sterilised jar and keep in the fridge. It is always nicer the next day!

MAKES ABOUT 600 ML

Easy onion marmalade

My last crop of onions was hopelessly too much, so after I gave away as much as my friends could take and still had enough for a season in the restaurant, I still had too many. So it was idea time.

This is an old yet easy Karoo recipe for a tasty onion marmalade that goes really well with venison and most meat dishes. It is sticky and sweet so will also do nicely with cheese and biscuits.

40 ml butter
750 g onions, thinly sliced
200 g soft brown sugar
150 ml red wine vinegar
15 ml mustard seeds

Heat the butter in a large, heavy-based pan and cook the onions for about 10 minutes, or until softened and lightly browned.

Stir in the remaining ingredients and cook, uncovered, for a further 25–30 minutes, stirring occasionally, or until the onions are lightly caramelised and very soft.

Ladle into hot sterilised jars and seal immediately. When cooled, refrigerate for up to 1 week.

MAKES ABOUT 2 X 500 ML JARS

Basil pesto

Basil pesto is not really a Karoo recipe, but I am going to get off this one on a technicality. You see, during the Second World War, plenty of Italian POWs were sent to the Karoo to work on farms. Many stayed on after the war ended and left a decidedly Italian slant to many Karoo dishes (see also page 104).

Pesto is so versatile and tasty that you can put it with most anything: cheese and biscuits, savoury snacks and anything else you may feel like.

1 large handful fresh basil leaves
125 ml olive oil
3 large cloves garlic
30 g pine nuts
Pinch of salt
125 g Parmesan cheese, grated

Place the basil, oil, garlic, pine nuts and salt in a blender and pulse until it forms a thick paste. Remove, add the cheese and serve.

Obviously it is best used freshly made, but you can top up with a thin layer of olive oil and store it in the fridge, in a sterilised jar, for up to a week.

MAKES ABOUT 250 ML

Recipe index
Page numbers in **bold** indicate photographs.

Baked goodies
   Aunty Maureen's marvellous muffins 156, **157**
   Cara McEwan's *mielie pap* biscuits 155
Beef 46–63
   Arno's rare spiced rump with mustard **54**, 55
   Beef casserole with parsnips and baby jacket potatoes **50**, 51
   Beef stir-fry with baby cabbage and seeds galore 52, **53**
   Easy-peasy shoulder roast 58, **59**
   Flash-fried *pap en sous* balls with Nguni mince 48, **49**
   Oxtail curry 60
   Rolled fillet stuffed with pine nuts, spinach and mushrooms 62, **63**
   Spade flambéed sirloin with mushrooms and asparagus 56
   Spicy crusted whole barbecued rump 55
   Two-buck chuck pot roast 61
Breads
   ASG's health bread 122, **123**
   Easy veldbraai beer bread **154**, 155
Burgers
   Lemon and thyme chicken burgers 78, **79**
   Venison burger patties **96**, 97

Charcuterie 104–117
   Cheesy warthog and herb sausage 116, **117**
   Fennel and lamb sausages 116
   Homemade smoked bacon 114, **115**
   Kirsten Short's cured venison sirloin 112

My own 'Farma' ham **110**, 111
Simple venison sausage 108, **109**
Spicy hunter's salami 113
Venison salami **106**, 107
Chicken 64–81
   Chicken breast roulade with fresh morogo and feta **74**, 75
   Chicken curry salad **80**, 81
   Chicken in goop 68
   Herby chicken pie **70**, 71
   Hole chicken 77
   Lemon and thyme chicken burgers 78, **79**
   One-pot chicken and veg casserole 69
   Slow-roasted basil chicken 66, 67
   Sunday roasted and brined chicken 72, **73**
   Wholegrain and herbed pancakes with creamy sage chicken filling 76
Curries
   Chicken curry salad **80**, 81
   Oxtail curry 60

Desserts (cold)
   Frozen hazelnut nougat **142**, 143
   Rum and raisin parfait **138**, 139
Desserts (hot)
   Baked almond creams 138
   Baked pancake roll with pear and brandy sauce **146**, 147
   Decadent chocolate and coffee soufflés **140–141**, 141
   Malva pudding 144, **145**
   Rose's winter comfort orange pudding 144

Lamb 28–29 *see also* Mutton
   Black pepper lamb casserole 40, **41**
   Chilli and pepper deboned leg of lamb on the braai 42, **43**
   Deboned shoulder of lamb and venison roasted with peaches, rosemary and thyme 44, **45**
   Fennel and lamb sausages 116
   Roasted lamb neck with fresh rosemary 36, **37**
   Rustic braised lamb shanks with beans **32**, 33
   Sticky ribs on the braai 34, **35**

Mutton 28–29 *see also* Lamb
   Classic roast leg of mutton 34
   Minty mutton summer stew 30, **31**
   Spicy mutton knuckles with garlic parsnip mash **38–39**, 39
   Sticky ribs on the braai 34, **35**

Offal
   Spicy venison tripe and trotters 99
Ostrich
   Slow-cooked one-pot neck stew 98

Pancakes
   Wholegrain and herbed pancakes with creamy sage chicken filling 76
Pasta
   Venison, Parma ham and mushroom lasagne 100, **101**
Pies
   Herby chicken pie **70**, 71
Pork
   Homemade smoked bacon 114, **115**
   My own 'Farma' ham **110**, 111

Preserves and seasonings
  Basil pesto 158
  Easy onion marmalade 158
  Mom's delicious pecan, apricot and peach conserve 152, **153**
  Wonder salt 151

Relishes
  Mango and chilli relish 94
  Natalie's lekker-hot bottled chilli relish **150**, 151

Roasts
  Classic Karoo roasted shoulder of springbok with homemade smoked bacon 90, **91**
  Classic roast leg of mutton 34
  Deboned shoulder of lamb and venison roasted with peaches, rosemary and thyme 44, **45**
  Easy-peasy shoulder roast 58, **59**
  Roasted lamb neck with fresh rosemary 36, **37**
  Slow-roasted basil chicken 66, **67**
  Sunday roasted and brined chicken 72, **73**
  Two-buck chuck pot roast 61

Salads
  Chicken curry salad **80**, 81
  Marinated prune and chilli salad with pistachio nuts and rocket **43**, 125

Sauces (savoury)
  Gravy 58
  Mild chilli sauce 93
  Raisin and Muscadel sauce 87
  Simple summer salad cream 156

Sauces (sweet)
  Pear and brandy sauce 147

Side dishes 118–135
  ASG's health bread 122, **123**
  Balsamic onions 93
  Crunchy seasonal veg with butter and salt 129
  Garlic parsnip mash 39, **39**
  Honey-glazed parsnips 130, **131**
  Magic potatoes **58**, 128
  Marinated prune and chilli salad with pistachio nuts and rocket **43**, 125
  Maryke's baked *pap* tart 124
  Mini potato bakes 126, **127**
  Oak-smoked mash 134
  Roasted beetroot with feta and fresh mint 135
  Rose's decadent savoury and sweet Christmas tart 120, **121**
  Seasonal green beans with roasted almonds and crispy bacon 130, **131**
  Stir-fried sweet potato with garlic, ginger and coriander **132**, 133
  Traditional morogo **132**, 133

Soup 16–25
  Blue cheese, biltong and port soup 24, **25**
  Carrot soup with orange and ginger 21, **21**
  Curried sweet potato and parsnip soup 20, **20**
  Elsanne's beetroot, onion and garlic soup **22**, 23
  Seven-bean classic Karoo boontjiesop 18, **19**

Stews and casseroles
  Beef casserole with parsnips and baby jacket potatoes **50**, 51
  Black pepper lamb casserole 40, **41**
  Chicken in goop 68
  Game bird potjie with oranges and ginger **102**, 103
  Minty mutton summer stew 30, **31**
  One-pot chicken and veg casserole 69
  Slow-cooked one-pot ostrich neck stew 98
  Spicy mutton knuckles with garlic parsnip mash 38–39, 39
  The ultimate hunter's stew with wild mushrooms and brown rice 88, **89**

Stir-fries
  Beef stir-fry with baby cabbage and seeds galore 52, **53**
  Stir-fried sweet potato with garlic, ginger and coriander **132**, 133

Tarts
  Maryke's baked *pap* tart 124
  Rose's decadent savoury and sweet Christmas tart 120, **121**

Venison 82–103
  Baked guinea fowl samoosas with a mango and chilli relish 94, **95**
  Baked wild hare spring rolls with raisin and Muscadel sauce **86**, 87
  Cheesy warthog and herb sausage 116, **117**
  Classic Karoo roasted shoulder of springbok with homemade smoked bacon 90, **91**
  Deboned shoulder of lamb and venison roasted with peaches, rosemary and thyme 44, **45**
  Game bird potjie with oranges and ginger **102**, 103
  Grey-winged partridge breasts with barley and baby peas 84, **85**
  Kirsten Short's cured venison sirloin 112
  Nadia Kitching's eland steak roll with mild chilli sauce **92**, 93
  Simple venison sausage 108, **109**
  Slow-cooked one-pot ostrich neck stew 98
  Spicy hunter's salami 113
  Spicy venison tripe and trotters 99
  The ultimate hunter's stew with wild mushrooms and brown rice 88, **89**
  Venison burger patties **96**, 97
  Venison salami **106**, 107
  Venison, Parma ham and mushroom lasagne 100, **101**